CONTENTS

LIST OF TABLES AND FIGURES   xi

ACKNOWLEDGEMENTS   xiii

PREFACE   xv

Chapter 1   **New Media and Electoral Representation**   1

The 47% Disaster, Data, and Information   1

How Citizens Make Good Political Decisions   4

A Shared Identity   4

Political Knowledge   5

Political Engagement   6

Being an Active Citizen   7

New Media and the Missing Utopia   9

Pussygate   14

The Brave New World   16

Suggested Readings   17

Chapter 2   **The American "Internet" Voter**   18

Who Is Howard Dean?   18

Digital Citizens: New Media Access   20

The Offline Adults   22

Online Access Points   28

Social Media Communities   29

The Cell Phone Revolution   31

Social Internet Adults   34

Digital Differences: New Media Use by the Political
American   37

The Online Political Person   43

Engaging the Politically Disinterested   45
Who Is Bernie Sanders?   47
Describing the American Internet Voter   48
Suggested Readings   51

Chapter 3   **Googling Political Information**   52
Following Football, Following Politics   52
Political Facts Versus Political Knowledge   55
The Internet, Learning, and Primary Elections   56
Individuals' Searching for Candidate Information
Online   62
Googling During the California Top Two Primary   65
Googling During Presidential Elections   67
Google and Democratic Values   69
Suggested Readings   72

Chapter 4   **Debating Politics in the YouTube
Comments Section**   73
Online Political Deliberation   75
Incivility and Perception   76
YouTube   79
Discussion Bubbles   85
Clinton Versus Trump Speeches: The YouTube
Commenters Community   86
Real Communication on YouTube   87
Suggested Readings   89

Chapter 5   **Receiving Tweets from Politicians**   90
Twitter in American Life   91
Tweeting Directly to Voters   93
The Tweeting President   97
Tweets That Connect   98
Twitter Bots, Popularity, and Fake News (Part 1)   99
The Psychology of Fake News   102
The Twitterverse and American Politics   103
Suggested Readings   104

Chapter 6   **Discussing Politics
Face(book)-to-Face(book)**   105
Facebook as a Force in Politics   106
Content of Shared Material   107
Who Are the Connectors?   109

Two-Step Flow: The Potential Magnitude of Sharing
    Politics Through New Media   110
Shared Memes   111
Online Sharing Occurs Less Frequently Than Actual
    Political Conversations   112
Fake News (Part 2)   113
Memes, Information, and Conversation: Political
    Conversation Between People Still Dominates
    New Media   115
Suggested Readings   116

Chapter 7   **Conclusion**   117
Better Consumers of News   119
Polarization and the Internet   121
    Reflection   122
Opportunities for Engagement and Further Thought   123

NOTES   125

BIBLIOGRAPHY   133

INDEX   141

LIST OF TABLES AND FIGURES

Tables

Table 2.1 Where Do You Get MOST of Your News about National and International-Issues?   28

Table 2.2 How Citizens Access News Online   29

Table 2.3 Social Media Use   30

Table 2.4 Political Activity in Social Media   30

Table 2.5 Use of Platforms to Post, Comment or Share Political News/Content   31

Table 2.6 Use of the Internet for Political News and Discussions, 2012   38

Table 2.7 How People were Contacted in 2012 for Collective Action   39

Table 2.8 Political and Collective Actions – Online vs. Offline   41

Table 2.9 Online Actors   44

Table 3.1 Presidential Primary Election Dates in 2008   61

Table 4.1 Top Level Comment Rate   81

Table 4.2 Top Level Comment Reply Rate   82

Table 4.3 Top Level Comment Like Rate   83

Table 6.1 Political Information Source (in the last two days)   108

Table 6.2 Shared Memes   112

Figures

Figure 2.1 Percentage of Offline vs Online Americans, 2000–2017   22

Figure 2.2 Online Adults, 2013   23

Figure 2.3 Offline Adults, 2016   25

Figure 2.4 Variables that Predict Internet Access   27

Figure 2.5 Online Adults   32

Figure 2.6 Cell Phone Online Adults   33

Figure 2.7 Online Social Adults – Twitter   35

Figure 2.8 Online Social Adults – Social Network Sites   36

Figure 2.9 Online Political Activities   42

Figure 2.10 Variables that Predict Political Internet Use 42
Figure 3.1 Google Search Volume for the Term: Vote, United States 67
Figure 3.2 Association Between State Search Volume for "Vote" and Voter
 Turnout in Presidential Elections 2012, 2008, 2004 68
Figure 3.3 Search Volume in the 2016 Presidential Primary
 in New Hampshire 69
Figure 4.1 Frequency of Specific User Comments for 2016 Presidential
 Announcement YouTube Videos 81
Figure 4.2 Reply Count for 2016 Presidential Announcement
 YouTube Videos 82
Figure 4.3 Like Count for 2016 Presidential Announcement
 YouTube Videos 83
Figure 5.1 Naive Bayes Comparison of Twitter and Roll Call Ideal Points 95
Figure 5.2 Misalignment 96
Figure 6.1 Meme Images 111

ACKNOWLEDGEMENTS

For their incredible patience as they waited for the genesis of an idea to grow into a manuscript we thank Mike Alvarez and Jennifer Carpenter. We have particularly benefited from conversations with Brian Rogers, Andy Sinclair, Ines Levin, Erin Hartman, Jonathan Nagler, Ethan Porter, and Vincent Bauer.

We would also like to thank the reviewers who provided us with feedback throughout this project: Bernard L. Bongang, *Savannah State University,* Philip Habel, *Southern Illinois University, Carbondale,* Tyler Johnson, *University of Oklahoma,* Martha Kropf, *University of North Carolina, Charlotte,* David Peterson, *Iowa State University,* and Hyun Jung Yun, *Texas State University.*

PREFACE

All around us are ordinary citizens reaching out to new media and engaging with political information. The man next to you on the bus reads today's *New York Times* on his smart phone as he commutes to his office. Your neighbors check their email and view a personalized message from their congressional representative to let them know his or her views on the issue of the day. Your friend updates her Facebook status, reads an article or two, and then shares a political meme that makes her laugh. Your professor Tweets a clever comment about a new article from *Politico*. Modern political communication frequently occurs through new media. What makes this type of communication different from traditional sources, such as print or television? New media are more than simply a new way by which information is distributed. The *on-demand* access of content provided by new media provides citizens with increased convenience to consume information, including information about politics. Moreover that access is frequently paired with *membership to an interactive user community*, where individuals can engage in discussions, post feedback, and create new content. The rise of the "alt-right" and their use of interactive media to communicate among like-minded members and to organize is an extreme example of how such a community can form, but one that has received extensive coverage in the media. New media changes the way citizens can interact with political information and with each other.

We define new media as media communication that provides on-demand access and that is frequently paired with membership to an interactive user community. Of course, we are primarily focused on the extent to which people engage with new media for politics. The rise of new media—and the convenience of political information—doesn't necessarily imply that people will automatically increase their political news diet. Indeed, the rise of new media implies that news about sports and entertainment is also more accessible, so politically uninterested citizens now have a larger menu to choose from for their favorite topics and they may inadvertently—or even deliberately—avoid politics in their news diet. The extent to which people consume politics via new media will be a key quantity to investigate. The most important role, though, that comes as a consequence of the rise of new media is in terms of the interactive user community. This is the place where new media really challenges the conventional view of how media influences political beliefs. Previously, media effects were seen as a consequence of elite political communication. Now, however, there are peer-to-peer media effects to consider, with the myriad of possibilities therein.

> **New Media:** Media communication that provides on-demand access frequently paired with membership to an interactive user community.

Does the presence of new media affect the average citizen's ability to responsibly bear the burdens of a participatory democracy? That is, does the American mass public use new media to become better citizens? The aim of this book is to address the question. This is an ambitious project, because this question is not easily answered with a single empirical illustration. We need to define what it means to be a good citizen. We need to evaluate the extent to which citizens consume political information via new media. Most importantly, we need to look at the effects of the user community on both an individual's level of political knowledge as well as level of political engagement and participation. In this project, we look to provide answers via distinct empirical illustrations: by focusing on one channel or one aspect of new media in each chapter, we are able to gain a better appreciation for the extent of the role of new media in the basic functions of democracy. These are some questions we consider: Who has access to new media and how are they using it? How does new media affect people's political knowledge? Do we see forums of deliberation online? Do we see constituents communicating with elected representatives online? How does new media compare to old media in terms of the sharing of political information? We provide evidence and answers for the following questions. We hope by building this body of knowledge we can answer our larger question as well: does the American mass public use new media to come better citizens?

1. Do citizens have equal access to the resources provided by new media? If they do have equal access, do they take equal opportunities to engage with new media for political purposes? Does the increased availability of information decrease societal cleavages about who is informed about politics?
2. Do we see evidence that the increased availability of information is used to make good electoral decisions? That is, does new media allow citizens to choose better representatives?
3. Does new media encourage more deliberation about policies, generating greater consensus?
4. Do we see elected representatives attune to constituents' concerns and communicating about their politics to their constituents via new media?
5. How do citizens talk to each other via new media?
6. How does new media compare to traditional media and politics?

As we address each of these questions, we focus on the ways in which new media enables citizens to engage with politics in a meaningful way. We also consider the risks involved: Each opportunity that citizens have for greater voice, greater reach, and greater engagement also requires greater responsibility. Americans have seen an expansion of their responsibilities since the founding of the country. Recall that until the 17th Amendment, US Senators were not elected by voters directly but instead were elected by the individual state legislatures. Nowadays institutions such as presidential primaries and ballot initiatives are designed to reflect the modern opinion that the average American citizen should have more voice in government. The rise of social media presents yet another opportunity for the expansion of American democracy. New media changes who, and what, makes the news: suddenly, ordinary citizens are in charge of the national political news agenda. Will citizens manage to use this new power well? Will their influence create good policy?

We argue that new media has changed the way an average citizen seeks, receives, and shares political information. Old media permitted more limited seeking of political information, old media required offline sharing, and old media required an intermediary, most of the time, for representatives to communicate to constituents. New media disrupts those processes: it drastically reduces the cost of searching for information, it permits online and immediate sharing with peers, and it permits representatives to communicate directly with constituents. We collect an array of illustrations from 2008 to 2016 to characterize the role of new media in each of these distinct processes. We argue that by illuminating these three behavioral processes, we are better able to understand the influence of new media on the quality of democratic engagement for an average citizen.

In a participatory democracy, the requirements of citizenship surpass that of obtaining the minimum necessary political information and knowledge to make good electoral decisions. Good citizens must be able to tolerate those who hold views that are different from their own and evaluate the credibility of those views. They also must know how to participate in a political process that holds political representatives accountable through active engagement. We see daily evidence that many citizens are seeking, sharing, and receiving political information through new media channels. However, a sizable part of the American population does not actively follow politics and the machinations of the political process. When we consider new media, we want to know if new media has had an effect on the ability of a democracy to function, and in particular we want to know if new media helps people become better citizens.

WHAT IS GOOD CITIZENSHIP AND HOW MIGHT NEW MEDIA PLAY A ROLE?

There are two distinct lines of argument regarding the role and effects of new media on political life in the United States (and internationally) that suggest the new media revolution may produce better citizenship. One argument suggests new media increases a sense of shared identity because it provides citizens with content created from an expanded set of authors, so that new media consumers then hear a broader array of opinions and have an increased appreciation of and toleration for the diversity of citizens in society. That is, better citizens are ones who have a better understanding of each other and their shared concerns. Citizens need a set of common experiences to adopt a shared identity, an allegiance to upholding common societal governance. A second argument describes the catalyst of new media as one that reduces the costs of obtaining political information. In a participatory democracy, being a responsible citizen requires a citizen to bear certain costs. For example, the capacity of citizens to observe and respond to government (in)action is closely linked to levels of government corruption and responsiveness. Governments that know that their citizens cannot or do not follow what they are doing often have little incentive to be responsible or honest. Citizens need access to political information and debates to form opinions. They also need opportunities for effective and informed participation (and, ideally, the desire to act on these opportunities). New media allows citizens to more easily bear the burdens of participatory democracy by making it easier to listen to others and to use new tools to procure the information necessary to guide effective engagement in politics. Reduced costs, increased flexibility, and greater availability of information permit a more diverse array of consumers to obtain political content. That is, better citizens are ones who are better informed. Further, more stable governance is advanced by increasing the voice of all people, which can be achieved by reducing the costs of information. Therefore, new media has the potential to generate a type of political person who can empathize with public interests and is an informed citizen.

There is ample evidence that new media allows citizens to more easily bear the burdens of participatory democracy by making it easier to listen to others and to use new tools to procure the information necessary to guide effective engagement in politics. We can see evidence of the effectiveness of the Internet as a participatory tool in authoritarian regimes around the world. An authoritarian regime is one where there is little formal political power relegated to the people; instead, political authority is concentrated by those not responsible to the citizens. Examples include Russia, Saudi Arabia, China, and Iran. Often authoritarian regimes regulate the Internet to limit access to information, and recent research has illustrated this happens with the aim of inhibiting the use of technology to overcome collective action problems. It is this latter point that is often the most important. Although most authoritarian countries do limit access to information online, these countries are often much more concerned about the use of the Internet for organizing protests. For example, in May 2016, a story circulated on Chinese social media of women and a child being beaten when they refused to leave houses scheduled for demolition. The government was not concerned about the story circulating—in fact, several officials were held accountable for the abuse—but if social media had encouraged Chinese to in front of the district mayor's office to protest, then the Chinese would have intervened and censored the message.[1] That is, what we can learn from the choices of authoritarian regimes is that the Internet is a tool that has the potential to be wildly successful at not only informing but also generating political action and participation.

A rival literature agrees that the Internet is effective in mobilizing people but argues new media creates two sets of problems. First, new media creates a society where there are two classes of people: the digital haves and the digital have-nots. The digital haves can access more information than the have-nots and can connect more easily than the have nots with the politicians, government agencies, interest groups, and media who are critical players in a democracy. The haves also coordinate their activities more easily because of their participation in online communities. The danger that these scholars see is that the digital haves will also be the people who are most likely to be politically active in the first place, ensuring that those who were already politically interested are now better off in terms of their ability to effectively engage in politics and those who previously had little interest in politics are less likely to participate. This danger is especially potent because the digital divide could follow and emphasize classic and disturbing societal and power cleavages that have existed across racial, educational, class, and even party lines. In short, new media channels reinforce power biases that have long existed in politics and even exacerbate them. If new media reduces the availability of common experiences and further divides the public based on their level of political interest, then the quality of the democracy will diminish. People may still be politically active, but they will not be participating in a joint effort to build a better society.

Critics of new media also argue that it is polarizing the population. These critics see interactive user communities being created online but they are gated communities, where entrance is not formally limited but is ideologically limited. This world is one where there is not a liberal or conservative community, but even narrower communities exist. The traditional "country club, Chamber of Commerce Republican" would find himself unwelcome in the liberal communities—where anti-vaccine, anti-GMO, and abortion rights viewpoints reign—but also in many of the Tea Party communities. His support for moderate change and pro-business activities would run afoul of Tea Party suspicions of free trade, immigration, and the potential for compromise. These narrow communities not only parrot a person's biases but also amplify and radicalize them, pushing people to become ever more firm in their stances. For these new media critics, the Internet creates a world where people do not hear opposing viewpoints, debate issues based on facts or research, or encounter people who hold other views. Instead, new media becomes an echo chamber.

This echo chamber is most perilous when the news is false. American politics has long been subjected to a steady undercurrent of conspiracy theories. A substantial and potentially growing number of citizens hold conspiratorial beliefs. For example, Oliver and Wood (2014), using four nationally representative surveys sampled between 2006 and 2011, find that half of the American public endorses at least one conspiracy theory. As Oliver and Wood (2014) argue, most political science research has presented media consumption as driven by elite discourse and political ideology, where political elites make statements that are picked up by media sources and then conveyed to citizens, who adopt beliefs largely conditional on their ideology and levels of political interest. Yet this model doesn't work when considering conspiratorial beliefs, which are largely absent from national dialogue. That is to say, many of these beliefs are communicated from one person to another. This kind of conspiratorial thinking can thrive in online communities, and polarized online communities that arise as a result of new media can be breeding grounds for whole new species of conspiracies and false stories. Some of these stories are commonly known: "President Obama was not born in the United States. Sandy Hook was a hoax. The Bush Administration knew about the 9/11 plot before it happened. John F. Kennedy was assassinated by the CIA" (Miller et al. 2015, 825). Miller et al. (2015) argue these conspiratorial beliefs are like to spread "horizontally"—that is, from one person to another—and that the development of conspiratorial beliefs is grounded in a fundamental psychological process called motivated reasoning, where individuals rely on their partisanship to process the cues around them. Here, people are motivated to "attribute nefarious intent to political opponents" (Miller et al. 2015, 826). Of course, not all fake news is conspiratorial in nature. What is true, however, is that the fake news and the conspiracy theories share a common adversarial thread, where like-minded individuals are perhaps more likely not only to share the story but also to adopt a common belief. Veritas and viral media are not well suited for each other.

We argue that good citizenship requires the development of a shared identity and the cultivation of active participation among citizens. New media has that potential. New media also poses risks in terms of creating a new kind of digital divide, based on political interest. It also may polarize beliefs within the population, and it poses risks in terms of the adoption of fake beliefs and the consumption of conspiratorial beliefs. This manuscript is designed to evaluate whether the new media revolution has been successful in improving citizenship and, if not, where the problems may be remedied.

THE COUNTERFACTUAL WORLD

There is evidence supporting each of these various theories about new media. The Internet is an amazing technology for spreading information and for learning, but it also can be a gated world that provides more ways for the politically engaged to become even more engaged. New media can create a common identity or create a common belief in conspiracy theory. What would the world be like without new media? What would an average citizen's political information diet look like without new media? It is hard to imagine a counterfactual: what does the world without new media look like? One thing to keep in mind when reading this book is the importance of the counterfactual. We need to imagine what would happen without this new resource. Imagine what the world would be like without the Internet. Quite a bit of research suggests that, even in the absence of the Internet, we would be living in a polarized society where the well-off were highly advantaged politically. Consider the following two examples.

First, even in the absence of the Internet, we would be living in a world where people were highly segregated by education and income. The Stanford Center for Education Policy Analysis has found that housing segregation has increased marked this century.[2] The rich and well educated live among the rich and well educated, and the poor live among the poor. In the 1970s, neighborhoods were more likely to have mixing, where lower-income people could afford to live in more middle-class neighborhoods and middle- and upper-class people were more mixed. Today, that mixing is much less likely to occur. So in a world without Internet, your conversations would still tend to be more with people like you, purely because you would be much more likely to interact with people with the same levels of education and income. You would not be likely to be exposed to other ideas through interactions with people having different life experiences.[3] People generate political ideas through groups: They do so in every conversation about politics specifically, they do so when they swap tales about morality and its violations, and they do so when they build up a sense of group identity.[4] The more these groups are demographically homogeneous, the more these groups will be homogeneous politically.

Second, the *Citizens United v. FEC* case would still exist and the landscape would be clearly tilted toward the rich and more politically active. *Citizens United* allows unlimited political spending by individuals, who would be able to engage in this spending without the transparency (albeit limited in many cases) that the Internet affords. Likewise, the ability of people like Senator Bernie Sanders to collect small contributions for his campaign would also be made much more difficult if the only way these contributions could be made was by writing a check or stuffing cash into an envelope and mailing it. The Internet has lowered barriers for regular people to contribute money to campaigns, using just a credit card.

What these examples illustrate is the power of connecting citizens. When citizens are connected both to information and to each other, political change is possible. Whether new media has been successful at empowering citizens, and whether it has successfully lowered the extent to which American political information is polarized, are questions we intend to address in this text. These are critical components toward building an answer to our question: does new media create better citizenship?

THE PLAN FOR THE BOOK: EXPLORING THE POLITICAL RAMIFICATIONS OF THE NEW MEDIA REVOLUTION

Whether new media can improve the quality of American citizenship is a question that does not have a simple answer. Answering a question this broad requires more specificity, starting with measuring a highly nuanced outcome (citizenship). Our project starts with a definition of good citizenship and describes some of the traits associated with a functioning and responsive democratic politic. Once we have a good set of metrics to evaluate citizenship, we can then consider questions of research design. Ideally we would identify both a population of citizens who have access to new media and their appropriate counterfactual—a similar population of citizens who do not have new media access. Ideally we would measure citizenship in both populations at several points in time—we would have collected metrics of good citizenship before the advent of new media and continued well after access was available to both, in order to measure how people transition to new media and when its influence on citizenship is felt and observed. Further, the population of individuals who adopted new media would be similar to those who didn't, ensuring that we could evaluate the effects of new media independent of traits such as socioeconomics and demographics. Unfortunately, this research design is mostly infeasible. These kind of empirical data are difficult to find if not impossible to find, and thus most scholarship on the influence of new media on citizenship has drawn conclusions about the effects of new media using more limited data resources. Our project suffers from similar limitations in terms of data. Yet, we have worked to employ as many relevant comparisons, to draw the right counterfactuals, as possible. We tell a story in pieces. We focus on a series of highly specific questions where each specific question addresses one aspect of new media or citizenship. We hope that by accumulating a number of smaller empirical illustrations the manuscript then generates a pattern of knowledge that builds toward the answer to the larger, more encompassing question about the effects of new media more broadly. This book focuses not only on who has access to new media but also on who is using it and for what purposes. It compares the range of citizenship metrics across new media channels. What it finds, then, is a nuanced picture of the relationship between new media and democratic citizenship.

This book does not aim to be a comprehensive evaluation of the relationship between new media and political engagement. Instead, we use various data to illustrate the various ways in which people are—and are not—using new media. In Chapter 1, we consider various theories related to new media, the potential benefits that may accrue from new media, and the problems it may create for democratic societies. In this chapter, we provide an overview of the possibilities—both positive and negative—that are possible in a world dominated by social media.

The chapters that follow examine specific theories regarding who uses new media and how it is changing politics. Ideally we would compare panel data on the political preferences, information-searching habits, and participation practices of individuals prior to and during the new media age. We would know which individuals transitioned to the digital world quickly, which individuals transitioned slowly, and which individuals never changed. Unfortunately, no such data exists. How then can we evaluate whether or not new media has helped the American mass public become better citizens?

Because we cannot compare the behavioral patterns of the same citizens before and after the advent of new media, we instead compare individuals who are similar in terms of their observed characteristics but who differ in terms of their patterns of use. We do this by drawing on and evaluating the significant body of existing survey data. In Chapter 2, we summarize the empirical data based on who does and does not have access to new media. We consider whether those differences are associated with differences in the use of new media for explicitly political purposes. In particular we pay attention to the classic social cleavages of race, class, and those relating to political interest. We break down the existing survey data on patterns of access and use to characterize the kinds of individuals who consume new media, paying particular attention to classic social cleavages such as race, gender, education, and age as well as political cleavages such as partisanship, knowledge, and interest. Using canonical survey data, we identify the extent to which particular subgroups of citizens are able to be involved in politics online and via new media. We provide an overview of the primary arguments related to the benefits and perils of new media in politics and provide a careful presentation of who benefits from the move toward new media and who does not. We then turn our particular focus toward three particular kinds of activities to demonstrate the relationship between new media, information, and engagement. Our key research questions considered in Chapter 2 are: (1) Are there digital divides—across racial/ethnic groups, educational attainment, age groups, and genders—that affect the potential for people to people to participate? (2) Are there certain new media that create smaller digital divides than other new media? and (3) How do levels of political engagement and information search vary across socioeconomic populations, assuming that they are online people?

After finding and describing differences in digital use, we illustrate the capacity of new media with four empirical analyses that form the basis of our argument for how new media may have improved the quality of citizenship. In Chapter 3, we show that, starting in the 2008 presidential primary elections in the United States, there was increased use of Google to search for information about the candidates in these primaries. This increased searching suggests that citizens do indeed leverage new media resources to become more informed. We also consider how voters search for information, what types of people do such searching, and on what digital platforms they search. We establish the ways in which elections change individual's searching patterns to incorporate searching for specifically political information by focusing on primary elections in the United States. We look for causal evidence that citizens rely on Google to search for candidate names ahead of primary elections. We find evidence of increased searching and believe this suggests citizens do indeed seek out information, particularly when they are unable to use other likely cues. In particular we are able to speak directly to the argument that only the information-rich get richer with new media and find that, in fact, a broad array of citizens are willing to conduct these searches, not only those who are already endowed with extensive political knowledge.

In Chapter 4, we provide evidence of a deliberative online citizenry. First, we document the presence of an online deliberative chamber through YouTube comments. We then consider the extent to which this information is discussed between citizens. We document the rate of comments across the 2016 presidential primary announcement videos, and then we expand this analysis to further understand variation in Trump and Clinton posters for their respective media channels. One important note, here, is simply to understand the norms of online engagement. There is a dark side to anonymous comments, and the quality of language and level of vitriol in online comments belies an unsophisticated and angry political community. Perhaps, then, deliberation online is not possible via these new media communities.

Chapter 5 considers how social media have given a new tool kit to political professionals. The use of websites, YouTube, Twitter, Facebook, blogs, and social connectivity programs like meetup.com has changed the way that campaigns communicate with voters. In this chapter, we first consider the supply side of new media in politics, focusing on how campaigns push information to voters. Specifically, we examine the ways in which members of Congress use technology to express themselves to their constituents. We find evidence that representatives deliberately communicate their ideology to their constituents directly through Twitter. We think these data suggest not only that candidates think their constituents want to know their ideology but also that candidates are now able communicate this information without the intermediary of classic media outlets.

In Chapter 6, we consider the sharing of information online, evaluating the extent to which constituents communicate to each other. How do people talk to each other online about politics? We pay particular attention to Facebook. We compare the rate of sharing online on spaces Facebook to other kinds of sharing. Social media platforms allow individuals to share political information in relationships where they otherwise would not have talked about politics. We evaluate the extent to which online sharing of political information parallels the kinds of sharing of social norms we know to change behavior. In particular, we focus on the power of a particular set of citizens—the opinion leaders online—to persuade their social connections. We illustrate the kinds of sharing that happens among citizens through new media. In particular we highlight how new media allows people to become more than consumers of content, ensuring that they can indeed both manipulate content (to create information) and link specific persuasive content to particular groups. We pay particular attention to those individuals who serve as public opinion leaders online, as these individuals are critical to helping the mass public evaluate online political resources.

In Chapter 7, we re-evaluate what kind of communication happens online, and the rate of online communication, and we compare this to the extent to which people are willing to talk politics to each other face-to-face. We evaluate what kinds of memes and norms individuals are willing to share through new media. We find strong evidence that new media encourages sharing, but more importantly we find that those individuals who are willing to talk about politics online are also frequently having offline conversations as well.

This book effectively summarizes who is using new media to communicate about politics. It provides several illustrations to suggest that some citizens are harnessing the power of new media to change the way they interact with politics. Although this book does not exhaustively demonstrate that all citizens have been affected by new media nor does it make the case for change in all kinds of politics and all kinds of behaviors, it does provide evidence explaining the relationship between new media and better citizenry. We hope that it inspires other scholars to add to this narrative and to challenge it as well. We also hope that this book engages readers to become more participatory citizens. Our illustrations suggest pathways to leverage new media to both obtain and disseminate practical political information. With these tools, citizens have the ability to engage more efficiently with the political process. Finally, one of our hopes is that this book will be used in the classroom. For interested students, we have included additional readings and descriptions of additional resources at the end of each chapter. Use them to expand your knowledge and build on the research we have started in this book!

A Connected America

Politics in the Era of Social Media

CHAPTER 1

New Media and Electoral Representation

THE 47% DISASTER, DATA, AND INFORMATION

New media can play a key role in shaping the way in which the public views political events. One example of a digital share affecting a candidate occurred during the 2012 presidential election, when comments by the Republican presidential nominee Mitt Romney at a private fundraiser at the home of a prominent donor, Marc Leder, became public. The quote illustrates important issues related to new media. Mitt Romney is quoted having said:

> There are 47 percent of the people who will vote for the president no matter what. All right, there are 47 percent who are with him, who are dependent upon government, who believe that they are victims, who believe that government has a responsibility to care for them, who believe that they are entitled to health care, to food, to housing, to you name it. That that's an entitlement. And the government should give it to them. And they will vote for this president no matter what. And I mean, the President starts off with 48, 49, 48—he starts off with a huge number. These are people who pay no income tax. Forty-seven percent of Americans pay no income tax. So our message of low taxes doesn't connect. And he'll be out there talking about tax cuts for the rich. I mean that's what they sell every four years. And so my job is not to worry about those people—I'll never convince them that they should take personal responsibility and care for their lives. What I have to do is convince the 5 to 10 percent in the center that are independents that are thoughtful, that look at voting one way or the other depending upon, in some cases, emotion, whether they like the guy or not, what he looks like.

Romney's comments went viral. Although they were first publicized by *Mother Jones* in a series of articles, what allowed the story to go viral and be shaped by new media was that a video of the comments was released with the story. The video could be seen on YouTube,[1] and this meant people could watch the video for themselves and hear the message *directly* from the candidate and assess his meaning for themselves. The Romney campaign could not claim that the comments were taken out of context; the video allowed everyone to see the comments in their entirety. Not surprisingly, after the video became public, the news media often referenced that Romney had said 47% of Americans were dependent on government.

Let's take a moment to consider why this quote was so powerful and what it tells us about how new media works. It reveals a great deal about the value of *new media* political information.

First, this quote was data that quickly became critical information. The comment Romney made occurred within the larger context of a presidential election campaign. Prior to this fundraiser, Romney had made tens of thousands of comments to groups and had taken positions on numerous important issues. This comment was just another data point in the larger context of the campaign. The transparency that the Internet provides is typically about just this—making data available to the larger public. These data just sit out in the ether until someone turns them into *information*. Data only become information when the data can be interpreted, when the data have a context that gives them meaning. (The term "big data" is often used to explain how large amounts of data can be combined and analyzed in order to find information and patterns.) According to one study, "from now until 2020, the digital universe will about double every two years."[2] This is an astounding number and it is likely that much of the data that will be produced over this time will just sit there, never being used to its full potential. The problem for the Romney campaign was that the comment reflected negatively on him. Many interpreted it to mean he did not care about a large part of the US population—"my job is not to worry about *those* people." It also occurred at a private event among wealthy donors, so was interpreted by some as being more authentic and honest; he made these comments without being concerned about pandering to the media. Critically, Romney's comments reinforced existing stereotypes about him: that he was rich and out of touch and only cared about people like him.

Second, information in the new media age can go viral. Once the story of Romney's comments was published by *Mother Jones*, it went viral, meaning it quickly circulated from person to person online, especially on Twitter. We discuss the new media platform Twitter in detail in a later chapter, but here it is sufficient to note that most people do not use Twitter to follow politics but most political elites and members of the media do. Once the story went viral in the new media world, it quickly went viral in other media contexts. The story became a fixture in print media, cable and broadcast news shows, and in conversations among regular people. Because almost all traditional media—from the *New York Times* to CBS News, to your local Fox News affiliate—also have new media components to their enterprises, the "viral" version of the story can appear on their website immediately and then more in-depth versions can appear in traditional news formats. This means that viral stories can keep reproducing and growing, as new facts lead to the story being updated and revised.

The Romney story went viral when *Mother Jones* first wrote about it, then again when the transcript of the event was released, and then again when the actual video was released.

Third, new media can be used to make information actionable. The Romney 47% quote is an example of information that became highly actionable. The quote was used by various actors—the campaign of President Barack Obama, groups allied with the Obama campaign, and individual supporters of President Obama—to mobilize people to support the Obama campaign. The number, 47%, quickly became a shorthand used by these groups for everything about the Romney campaign, and it was used to define who Romney was. In commercials, social media posts, news stories, and other places, 47% was used to explain why people should support Obama.

To summarize, then, why did the 47% story matter? Romney's 47% comment illustrates the interaction between engaged online citizenship, the desire of elites to communicate directly to citizens without engaging traditional media, and the power of individuals to talk to each other online. Engaged online citizens consumed this information as they sought information to determine their candidate choices for the upcoming presidential election. Social media allowed the story to be shared by traditional media and also by ordinary people. As this story spread, it formed the basis of political deliberation. Finally, and importantly, it allowed the candidate—Romney—to speak directly to the voters via this video. Although his campaign surely did not want this message broadly shared, there was indeed an impact from being able to hear the candidate communicate his 47% message himself. Seeking, sharing, and receiving new media potentially imply that a leaked video can destroy a presidential campaign faster than ever before, maybe in a way that wasn't possible prior to the new media revolution. But does that capability make democracy better? New media improves democracy only if accumulating and sharing this information truly improves the decision-making of citizens.

Seeking, receiving, and sharing information in this way challenges the conventional understanding of who makes the news. In both the economic model of news, where skilled professionals put together a news menu designed to maximize audience reaction, and the organizational model, where the news menu is negotiated between journalists, sources, and professional news organizations, there is little space for the news to be actively produced by citizens. Indeed, even the civic journalism model is driven by elites: elites discern the preferences of citizens and then devise a news menu accordingly (Graber and Dunaway 2015). In none of these models are the primary drivers of the news *ordinary citizens*. This is what new media challenges: new media allows citizens to decide what is critical information, what is going to be shared and made viral, and what actions need to be taken. Indeed, evidence that this new model—the new media model—is rampant is the very fact that legislators and elected officials are increasingly directing their communication straight to those citizens.

One thing you will see in this book is that we use examples from elections going back to 2004. There are many reasons for this—sometimes that is when an experiment was conducted or when the best data are available for the phenomena being described. What is important to recognize is that the behaviors being described still apply today (yes, even in the world of Trump!).

HOW CITIZENS MAKE GOOD POLITICAL DECISIONS

American government is structured as a republic, not a direct democracy. In a republic, citizen self-government is achieved by deliberative and informed participation designed to advance not merely a citizen's self-interest but rather the common interests of all who are governed (Sunstein 2007). As Sunstein (2007, 33) writes, "the founders placed a high premium on the idea of 'civic virtue,' which required participants in politics to act as citizens dedicated to something other than their own self-interest, narrowly-defined." To fulfill their obligations, citizens need to develop three attributes: (1) a shared identity, (2) a knowledge of the issues facing society, and (3) active engagement in civic life.

A Shared Identity

Sunstein argues that a shared identity is developed through common exposures to debate in newspapers, magazines, and television. Developing a shared identity has become more and more difficult over the past 20 years, and new media has played only a small role in this change. When a person turned on a television 40 years ago, there were three networks—CBS, NBC, and ABC (Fox was not a network yet)—and the top-rated television shows were seen by between 17 million and 20 million people, or 25% and 30% of all households. Today's top-rated television shows are seen by the same total number of viewers, but there are now twice as many households, meaning that the top shows are seen by less than 20% of Americans. Also, because television was still relatively new 40 years ago, people often watched the evening news over dinner—the news was the only programming on between 5:30 and 7:30 pm. People who otherwise wouldn't watch the news still often saw it because the television was on. This gave a broad segment of American society a common experience that helped build a shared identity. Focusing just on television, the media environment is completely different compared to 40 years ago; the number of viewing options between 5:30 and 7:30 pm is exponentially higher than it was 30 or 40 years ago. This change means that people who would rather watch entertainment can avoid the news and watch something on one of the hundreds of other television channels (Prior 2005, 2007).

The traditional media environment is also different in many other ways compared to the 1970s or 1980s. Today, we have radio options that didn't exist 40 years ago, like National Public Radio or daily talk radio shows that have a specific ideological bend, à la Rush Limbaugh or Sean Hannity. Until the early 1990s, newspapers remained a dominant source of information as well—and the daily delivery of the paper signaled the arrival of the day's media narrative. Today, the three traditional media—television, radio, and print news—have become a small part of a much larger universe of Internet news sources. (For political junkies, Axios and Politico specialize in the tick-tock of American politics). The news junkie does not have to wait for the evening news to find out what happened today. Even if a person loves to watch the news, there are several 24 hour news channels on cable television and a person can stream news from around the world—the BBC, Russia Today, Al Jazeera—if they do not like the American options. For people who are not news junkies, they can avoid being caught up in the news entirely except for seeing headlines as they check their email or search for their entertainment content of choice. Because there are so many news outlets, even news junkies may not be getting the same daily news narrative because they are getting information from different sources that bring a different bend to the news. Although developing a shared identity is more difficult, it is still possible.

Through the late 1980s, many major cities had at least two newspapers, one that published in the morning and one that published in the afternoon. Starting in the 1950s with the rise of the evening news broadcast on television, the afternoon newspapers slowly began to die off. This is yet another example of how new media are *not* unique. Radio and television were disrupters long before there was an Internet, and the rise of cable television was a disrupter to traditional broadcast media before the Internet as well. Ironically, the rise of the Internet has led to the return of the afternoon newspaper. In 2014, the *Washington Post* provided a morning and afternoon download service to users of the Amazon Fire tablet.

Political Knowledge

Once citizens have a shared identity, they still need to acquire sufficient *political knowledge* to make reasoned political choices. This does not necessarily mean that voters need to be filled with an encyclopedia of political facts to make informed decisions: a growing literature suggests that such encyclopedic knowledge does not necessarily correspond with real political knowledge (Graber 1984; Popkin 1994; Lupia 1994, 2006; Lupia and McCubbins 1998; Gibson and Caldeira 2009; Boudreau 2009). Political scientists typically measure such knowledge by asking if people can name the Speaker of the US House of Representatives, the Chief Justice on the US Supreme Court, and other factual questions. It turns out that voters need very little political knowledge to make informed choices; there are multiple conditions under which people can make competent decisions despite lacking fact-based answers to the standard political knowledge questions. Many, if not most, voters are able to make voting decisions based on very simple cues. For example, in a study of voting on five California ballot referenda in 1988 (pre-Internet) related to a complex set of insurance reforms, researchers found that all that a voter needed in order to make an informed choice was to know the preference of key interest groups (in this case, trial lawyers, the insurance industry, or the consumer activist Ralph Nader). Voters who were otherwise not following the politics of insurance reform but who knew the preferences of the insurance industry voted very similarly to voters who were closely following the issue and who knew the insurance industry's preferences (Lupia 1994).

Today, gathering political information is very easy—it is only a click away on the computer. However, people are not always adept at ensuring that the information that they collect is actually factual and reliable (Calfano and Kruse 2016). People may read online that a position is endorsed by someone they trust, but the source of the endorsement may be unreliable and may have the information incorrect. Even people who seek out information may think it is coming from a reliable source and not realize that the source has very specific biases. For example, many think tanks in Washington, DC, serve as fronts for special interests but one would not know this from the names of the organizations.[3]

Political Engagement

Good citizens also need to be able to transform their new political knowledge into *political engagement*. Empirically there is a strong association between political knowledge and political action, but whether an increase in political knowledge results in an increase in political action is far less clear. What we do know is that many forms of political action are easier than they have ever been. People can contribute to campaigns using their computer and a credit card in just a few minutes, or in a few seconds using pay-by-text technologies. People can also use online apps, such as Crowdpac, which has people take a short online quiz about their political interests and matches them up with candidates who share their ideology and to whose races they can contribute.[4] People can evangelize about a candidate or issue on Facebook or Twitter, they can sign a petition, send an email to their political representatives or government agencies, comment on a new federal rule, and even register to vote.

Targeting: One thing that is important to keep in mind about political engagement is that politicians and interest groups do not want everyone to participate. They only want people who support their positions and viewpoints to participate. Marketing consultants do extensive data analyses to determine who should be targeted with direct marketing messages—via email, social media advertising, or direct mail. One key component of this targeting is a person's voter history. Younger Americans are much less likely to be registered to vote than other Americans and are also less likely to have a voting history. Because they do not have a vote history, they are also less likely to be targeted by political parties or interest groups with materials intended to mobilize their voting.

Political engagement is also easier because it is now easier than ever for political campaigns and interest groups to target people and encourage them to participate. Much of your life—the groups you "like" online, your memberships to groups from the National Rifle Association to the World Wildlife Fund, your voting history, attributes of the zip code where you live, and a myriad of other factors—exist in data files that can be and are aggregated and then used by candidates and interest groups to target you so that you will engage in politics, give money, join their group, and give money (groups really want your money!) This targeting can be tested to determine which email subject lines work best, which targeted Facebook ad grabs your attention, and which Google search ad piques your curiosity. Data analytics (what used to be called statistics) is used to optimize targeting, presenting you with the best marketing materials possible. These analytics are also used to identify which households should be visited by political canvassers. It is important to remember that, for all of the contacting that can be done online, the most effective persuasion is done face-to-face.

When Alexis de Tocqueville visited the United States in the 1830s, he noted that Americans like to belong to groups that help them achieve their goals. Often, we take it for granted that there are groups to serve all needs and that such diversity is good. Yet, this diversity can generate enormous conflict. The Founding Fathers recognized this when they wrote the *Federalist Papers*. There, they noted that one of the biggest threats to American society was the existence of political factions, or groups. People naturally want to join groups and are drawn to people with similar interests, or passions. In general, they also want the groups to which they belong to be privileged in the political world. Bicyclists want more bike lanes. Individuals with disabilities want better services for their community members. Problems can occur when groups engage in factional politics, where they do not recognize that other groups also have interests, or use their power to oppress less powerful groups.[5] Today, there are interest groups that represent various interests, and many of these groups make a point of taking data that are reported online and turning those data into information. For example, *www.opensecrets.org* takes data regarding campaign finance, lobbying, independent expenditures by political organizations, and similar data and does two important things with it. First, they take the data and turn it into useful information, in the form of blog posts, reports, and news releases. Second, they create online "widgets" that the public can use to find data they can use to inform themselves about politics. If a person is not sure they agree with how *www.opensecrets.org* has presented something, the person can use these widgets to examine the data themselves. Group politics has led to the generation of a myriad of interest groups which can then map data into useful information for their members.

Being an Active Citizen

All of these data and this information can and do promote transparency. However, for new media to transform politics and governance, citizens must be willing to be attentive and use this information to learn more about what government is doing.

Most critically, this kind of accountability revolution requires all citizens—not just a small set of activists—to leverage this new information for political action. Arguably, organized interest groups improve the quality of democracy by expanding access to political data. By letting members know about the behavior and actions of government, particularly when these actions are relevant for members, these groups increase citizen supervision of government. This, then, gives us a framework to understand the kinds of changes that are possible with a new media revolution. New media are responsible for decreasing the costs of government supervision through increased and more efficient access to public records of government activity and digested information about these activities. **Citizens are then responsible not only for collecting and distributing this information but also for acting on this new information. Through their actions, citizens can ensure that the government is held in check.**

Shared identity, political knowledge, and political engagement are three key tenets of good citizenship. The development of the Internet generally has been seen by many as having great prospects for improving citizenship and civic engagement. One reason why is that, in an idealized world, the Internet has the potential to be a place where citizens can expound on issues and engage in informed debate. Habermas (1989) argued that a public sphere is a place in social life where all citizens are able to come together—not as business people or professionals engaging in personal transactions or as politicians bounded by the state but as citizens discussing matters of general interest.

In the public sphere, public debates and discussions on any issue or topic can occur, public opinion and general public agreement can be shaped, and decision-making can occur. The development of public spheres come in part from the formulation of rights in constitutions. Habermas writes:

> In the first modern constitutions the catalogues of fundamental rights were a perfect image of the liberal model of the public sphere: they guaranteed the society as a sphere of private autonomy and the restriction of public authority to a few functions. Between these two spheres, the constitutions further insured the existence of a realm of private individuals assembled into a public body who as citizens transmit the needs of bourgeois society to the state, in order, ideally, to transform political into "rational" authority within the medium of this public sphere. The general interest, which was the measure of such a rationality, was then guaranteed, according to the presuppositions of a society of free commodity exchange, when the activities of private individuals in the marketplace were freed from social compulsion and from political pressure in the public sphere (Habermas et al., 1974).

In the pre-Internet world, such discussions could easily be held, but only in a localized setting. Individuals in Odessa, Texas, and Nashua, New Hampshire, could both hold town meetings to discuss the same issue. However, these discussions would reflect the distinct views on a given issue that exist in New Hampshire or Texas. Before the advent of new media, it would have been difficult to bring together people and information together across the vastness of the United States (or any country of any size). Pre-Internet, a town hall meeting in New Hampshire and one in Texas could not easily share information and attitudes in real time. Today, technology can allow communities of individuals to be exposed to the same information about an issue, vote on various options related to the issue, and contribute their own information and knowledge to this debate. People in Texas and people in new Hampshire can have the same conversation, interactively, because of technology and social media. Technology means that people are no longer limited by time and space in their ability to contribute to a debate. In this idealized model, good citizenship is enhanced because more individuals are able to engage in ways that build political knowledge and a shared identity.

So have new media resulted in improved citizenship or has the public sphere continued to deteriorate, taken over by interest groups and manufactured public opinion, things that Habermas himself saw occurring in modern societies?

NEW MEDIA AND THE MISSING UTOPIA

As just described, new media would seem to be the basis for a political utopia, one where everyone can contribute to political debates and participate in the generation of political knowledge. So, now 20 years since the advent of the modern Internet, where is this utopia? Scholars generally suggest that there are four reasons new media have not revolutionized politics and improved citizenship:

- First, although information searching and acquisition costs are very low online, this decrease in cost has primarily benefited the wealthy and well educated (the individuals who already sought out information and have continued to do so)—those citizens who were already well informed about politics.
- Second, a more informed citizen is not necessarily able to make better political decisions, especially if individuals are merely seeking out specific information that supports and reinforces their own biases.
- Third, there may be no relationship whatsoever, or at least a tenuous one at best, between informedness and actual political engagement.
- Fourth, changes in society that have occurred offline have made the American political landscape very different today than it was in the past, and these changes help explain, in part, the current political climate and public engagement.

There are disagreements in the academic literature as to the validity of each of these statements. One of the goals of this book is to understand the kinds of arguments that researchers have espoused and then to think carefully about the kinds of questions we can and cannot answer empirically to provide additional evidence in this debate. Let's explore each of the listed arguments in turn.

Do new media primarily benefit the wealthy and increase the information gap between more-informed and less-informed citizens? In considering this question, it is important to consider that the fundamental distinction that is drawn between the well-informed and less-informed is that of interest and skill. Those citizens who are already more informed about politics have higher levels of political interest and have greater capacity to obtain new information, either because of additional education or other resource differences (Sniderman et al. 1991). As Brady et al. (1995) have noted, levels of educational attainment and income explain much of the differences in participation. As Meredith Rolfe (2012) has noted, there is a large social component to political participation; individuals with college degrees are much more likely to participate in such discussions and therefore feel social incentives to become involved, compared to individuals who do not have a college degree. Participation differences are exacerbated further because the well-off also develop more civic skills at work, in religious institutions, and in social organizations and these skills translate to even higher levels of participation. New media, much like civic skills, could exacerbate differences in participation between different groups.

The counterargument is that citizens share information and in particular will seek out peers with political expertise or engage members of their social network (Huckfeldt and Sprague 1995; Schlozman et al. 2013). Thus, informing some of the citizenry has an indirect effect on the rest of the population. Given that people can make decisions based on limited amounts of information, even if only some people are using new media to gather information, those people can serve as hubs, educating their social networks and potentially motivating them to participate in politics. Additionally other scholars argue that decreasing the costs of information has the potential to expand access to political information or even the construction of political communities by removing restrictions based on geography or time constraints (Putnam 2000; Dahl 1989; Etzioni 1993).

As Schlozman et al. (2010) argue, the future may be one where new media changes the ways in which individuals participate in politics. However, this change has not occurred yet. Using data from 2008, they find

> little evidence that there has been any change in the extent to which political participation is stratified by socio-economic status, but [that] the web has ameliorated the well-known participatory deficit among those who have just joined the electorate. Even when only that subset of the population with Internet access is considered, participatory acts such as contributing to candidates, contacting officials, signing a political petition, or communicating with political groups are as stratified socio-economically when done on the web as when done offline. The story is different for stratification by age where historically younger people have been less engaged than older people in most forms of political participation. Young adults are much more likely than their elders to be comfortable with electronic technologies and to use the Internet, but among Internet users, the young are not especially politically active.

Does new media provide citizens with the right information—and common information—to make better political decisions, information that does not merely reinforce existing biases? New media would seem to be a panacea for improving access to political information. Theoretically, new media could increase the number of shared experiences a person can have and also increase the base level of political information. Assuming a person can get online, the amount of political information they can access is vast. However, as Negroponte (1996) and other authors have argued, the benefits of the vastness of information on the Internet should not be overestimated. What is required to make information on the Internet consumable is the ability to search for it, and search inevitably results in a winnowing process. Everyone has limits on their time, and so they have to tailor their information search efforts.

To understand what this tailoring means for politics today, it is important to consider how Americans had shared experiences related to news and political information prior to the advent of the Internet. Markus Prior (2005, 2007) has examined this question extensively and finds that the American public had a relatively similar shared news experience prior to the advent of the widespread adoption of cable television, the Internet, and social media. Remember, it was not until the mid-1980s that 50% of US households had cable television and, even then, the only cable news channel was CNN. As Prior notes, when there were three primary news networks—ABC, CBS, and NBC—viewers tended to turn on the television to their network of choice and leave it on for extended periods.[6] As Prior (2005, 579) notes,

> since broadcast channels offered a solid block of news at the dinner hour and again after primetime, many viewers were routinely exposed to news even though they watched television primarily to be entertained. . . . Once exposed to television news, people learn about politics. Although a captive news audience does not exhibit the same political interest as a self-selected one and therefore may not learn as much, research on passive learning suggests that even unmotivated exposure can produce learning. According to Graber (1988, 114), "[p]eople who are exposed to large amounts of news will remember many stories despite lack of interest because mere exposure produces learning."

This active or passive news uptake was also quite widespread. According to Prior (2007), 75% of all households with a television on in the early evening were watching one of the three broadcast news channels, giving most Americans a common understanding of politics and the news. This common experience meant that liberals, conservatives, and everyone in between had a common set of information from which to work when considering political issues.

Compare this common experience to the world today. With the Internet, you can search for information that fits your personal biases. Instead of a common experience, the Internet (along with the segmentation of news on cable) allows people to filter information exposure so extensively that new media creates an echo chamber. Negroponte (1996) and Sunstein (2001, 2007) have referred to this concept as a "Daily Me."

- If you are liberal-minded, your daily me might start by going onto your iPad or smart phone and looking at the *HuffingtonPost*, skimming *DailyKos*, checking out other liberal news aggregators like *Thinkprogress*, and maybe looking at part of the *New York Times* before flipping over to *Slate.com* later.
- The conservative-minded can start their day off on *Redstate.com* and *DrudgeReport*, then flip over *The Daily Caller* before flipping over to *Fox News*.

In the world of the "Daily Me" a liberal and a conservative may both read about the same news events, but the discussion and framing of the stories are likely to be very different. Negroponte (1996) noted that this sort of information segregation could undermine the common experience that is critical in a democratic society. There is no longer a common understanding of the issues of the day. The American public is divided into separate liberal and conservative audiences for politically oriented books seen via the Amazon.com "also-bought" lists (Krebs 2004), and into separate liberal and conservative audiences for blogging networks (Adamic 2005), and the concern more generally is that the American public is dividing into separate liberal and conservative groups who have little opportunity to engage with each other's political beliefs. How, then, can we support the ideals of a participatory democracy?

Others scholars have found that new media allow people to experience a freedom to explore ideas that they might not otherwise seek out, for example, because of fear of violating community political norms. The Internet allows people to search and engage in debate anonymously, removing the social constraints and awkwardnesses associated with political disagreement and allowing people to gain greater exposure to different viewpoints (Gentzkow and Shapiro 2011). Consider, for example, a person who is liberal and lives in a very conservative community. Before there were new media, this person would have to go to a bookstore to buy books or magazines that were of interest to them, and people in the community might talk about their readings and political leanings. Using new media, they can explore a broader range of views and engage in discussions that are more diverse than the conversations they can have in their own community, and they can do so without stigma. For example, Seth Stephens-Davidowitz has used data from Google searches to show that there are pools of very liberal activists located in relatively conservative states—Alaska, Idaho, and Montana—and these individuals use the Internet to learn more about issues of interest to activists (e.g., Green Party candidates and impeaching President Trump) that would have been difficult to do in an analog era.

Does new media exposure result in increased political participation? New media does facilitate easier participation in some domains (in particular for campaign donations and contacting public officials). However, researchers have generally concluded that, despite these lower barriers for participation, political participation has not dramatically increased since the advent of new media (Bimber and Davis 2003; Bimber 2001, 2003; Jennings and Zeitner 2003). Instead, it appears that participation has largely shifted from the analog, "old media" world to new media.

For example, according to the Pew Research Center, "between 1996 and 2007 the proportion of Americans who reported that the Internet was one of their two most important sources of campaign news rose from 2 to 26 percent; at the same time, the proportion who made the equivalent assessment of newspapers as a source of campaign news declined from 49 to 30 percent" (Scholzman et al. 2013, 488).

Schlozman et al. (2013) present an interesting and nuanced picture of the online political world. As would be expected, the wealthy and well-educated use the Internet to participate in politics—activities such as contributing to candidates, contacting elected officials, signing political petitions, or communicating with political interest groups—more than do the less well off and less well educated. However, the historical experience of younger people being less engaged in politics may slowly be changing because of the Internet. Younger people have grown up online and use applications such as Twitter, Facebook, and similar social media more often than people who are older. Compared to those over 30, people 18 to 29 who use social media were more likely to have posted their own comments about political or social issues, more likely to have posted links to political stories, and more likely to have encouraged others to take action on a political or social issue. This shift toward new media as a key source of political information and as a medium for certain types of participation has the potential to construct different political communities, depending on who is using these media. However, the data on electoral turnout, especially in mid-term elections, do not suggest that the use of social media has boosted voting rates by any appreciable amount.

How is American society different today compared to the recent past? Although it is easy to blame the Internet—especially social media—for the current state of American politics and political engagement, many changes would have occurred without the Internet. For example, the difficulties of creating a shared identity through a common narrative that came through shared news exposure occurred prior to the Internet. The explosion of cable television and the rise of talk radio and public radio occurred prior to the advent of the Internet. The decline in trust in political institutions in the United States dates back to the 1960s. The polarization of the political parties was occurring in the 1980s and early 1990s. People have also had a life that had aspects of a "daily me" caused solely by the history of racial segregation in the United States, especially housing segregation.

This is not to say that the Internet has not played a role in the current issues associated with being a good citizen. The Internet clearly does make it easier for people to avoid being a part of a common narrative that makes for a shared American identity, and it clearly makes it easier to find more "facts" to support one's position, whatever that position may be. But the Internet also has made it easier to engage in politics and for interest groups and candidates to mobilize you to participate in politics.

New media has increased the potential for transparency in politics. The actions and words of political representatives, governmental organizations, and even many interest groups are recorded, digitized, and stored, making some of the most isolated political moments publicly distributable and immediately accessible. The former US senator George Allen (R-VA) became the example case of this in 2008, when a passing comment he made, calling a political operative for the his opponent a "macaca," created a political firestorm that helped to undermine his campaign.[7] The former US representative Anthony Weiner (D-NY) had to resign from office—and his candidacy for mayor of New York sank—when inappropriate photo shares he had sent over his Twitter account became public. New media can also create firestorms among interest groups when politicians cosponsor or support controversial legislation, something that Senator Bob Bennett (R-UT) experienced in 2009 and 2010, when Tea Party groups targeted his re-election campaign.[8]

Proponents of government transparency also laud the rise of new media as something that can revolutionize government accountability and promote more effective governance. Today, people can find any proposed federal regulation and the comments that have been submitted related to any proposed rule on *regulations.com*. It is possible to track federal spending related to the American Recovery and Reinvestment Act (the 2009 stimulus bill) and Hurricane Sandy relief efforts on *recovery.gov*. Federal contacts and assistance can be tracked at *fedspending.org* and at *usaspending.gov*. Campaign finance data can be analyzed at *opensecrets.org*. Data for citizens to monitor the actions of government, it seems, are everywhere.

PUSSYGATE

Not everything that is viral about politicians is necessarily disruptive to standard politics. The 2016 election had a bombshell event involving a recording of a candidate—also a Republican presidential candidate—but this one ended quite differently than the Romney story. This second example is very similar to the Romney illustration, where a presidential candidate was privately recorded and unknowingly so, but then the recording was disturbing to the public—and this second story allows us to illustrate why the ubiquitous sharing associated with new media doesn't necessarily change public opinion or serve as a politically disruptive voice.

On October 7, 2016, the *Washington Post* released a video from 2005 where Donald Trump was doing an appearance on *Access Hollywood* and was talking to the interviewer, Billy Bush, in what Trump thought was an off-mic conversation. During this conversation, Trump began bragging about his sexual exploits and was recorded saying, "I don't even wait. And when you're a star, they let you do it, you can do anything . . . grab them by the pussy."[9] The initial *Washington Post* story about this generated 29,400 comments on its webpage and the accompanying YouTube video was viewed 151,448 times. Like the Romney story, this quote was data that quickly become critical information. People could watch the video for themselves—that is, again they could hear the message *directly from the candidate*. Like the Romney story, this was information that quickly went viral. The story became a fixture in print media, in cable and broadcast news shows, and in conversations among regular people.

What is so interesting about the Trump "grab them" story is that the story had a very different affect on the 2016 campaign compared to the Romney 47% comment four years earlier. First, the reaction of political elites, particularly Republican elites, was quite different. A subset of Republicans disavowed Trump, but the majority of Republican representatives did not. The expected backlash didn't occur: Republican leaders ranging from Senate Majority Leader Mitch McConnell, to vice-president candidate and running mate Mike Pence, to Republican National Committee Chairman Reince Priebus were unflinching in their support of Trump's candidacy. There were a handful of Republicans who did cease supporting Trump (John McCain, for example), but mostly the Republican Party was unswayed by the video revelation. Second, this revelation didn't effectively sway public opinion: YouTube viewers clicked "thumbs up" more times than "thumbs down" on the video (431 to 319), and public opinion polls demonstrate the revelation had little effect on Trump support. According to a news report on Slate.com,

> CBS/YouGov conducted its battleground state polling of registered voters in Ohio, Pennsylvania, and Wisconsin from Oct. 5 through Oct. 7 and then "recontacted" participants in Ohio and Pennsylvania on the Oct. 7 and Oct. 8 to ask them about the recording. Among Trump supporters who had heard about the tape, 91 percent in Ohio and 90 percent in Pennsylvania said "the tapes have had no impact on their view of Trump." Eight percent of Trump supporters said the tape makes them think less of Trump, while two percent . . . think more highly of him.[10]

As further evidence that there wasn't a strong public opinion response to the Trump tape, the Clinton campaign didn't produce a response ad to the story until November 1st, when Trump's words were replayed along with other accusations from women who accused him of sexual assault.[11] The ad also included other quotes, such as recordings of Trump saying sexist statements such as, "putting a wife to work is a very dangerous thing" and that if dinner isn't ready when he comes home "I go through the roof."

Although this recording was as widely shared as the Romney video we described at the start of this chapter, it does not appear to have had the same impact as the Romney video. There is no definitive research on why the Trump video did not have a strong negative effect on his campaign, but there are differences between the videos that provide possible explanations. First, the Romney video occurred contemporaneously to the campaign but the Trump video occurred 11 years earlier. Second, the Romney video was highly policy specific. It described how he viewed a large segment of the population and also how he might treat people if he were elected. If you felt as though you were part of the 47%, Romney's comment felt like a personal attack on you. The Trump video spoke to Trump's character and demeanor, and people could interpret his motives for making the comments differently. Many Trump supporters argued his comments were "locker room banter among guys" and were not meant to be taken literally or seriously. Third, the Trump video was released during what was a much more kinetic election compared to 2012, where there were many more news narratives occurring on a daily basis. This cacophony of information may have made it more difficult for any one story to resonate in the same way as it might have in 2012. Finally, the Trump video may not have provided new information for many people; although the language and details contained in the video were new, similar stories had already been published.

THE BRAVE NEW WORLD

We live in a brave new world, one that presents both opportunities and challenges to America. The challenges are clear: it is easier than ever to avoid being a part an ongoing, common conversation about what is going on in society. For some people, the conversation is about politics, the current economic conditions, and global controversies. For some people, the conversation is about the fate of a set of "Real Housewives," Justin Bieber's new tattoo, and Beyonce's new song. Often these two groups do not intermingle. Moreover, even people who care about politics and the economy may not be a part of a common conversation. Some may be having a conversation that is occurring on one set of television, talk radio, and new media channels, and others are having a conversation on a different set of television, radio, and new media channels. Once the proliferation of media began in the 1980s with the broad adoption of cable television, these differences existed without the Internet. They may be discussing the same topics but using an entirely different set of information and presented with very different points of view. All of these outlets for information and different topics of conversations leave people flooded with information.

It is important to remember that the rise of new media is part of a larger explosion of information—on television, on radio, and online. In the political context, political information has never been more easily accessible, and the Internet allows citizens to seek out relevant information for themselves. In fact, social media can make this information-gathering process simpler. If I follow key opinion leaders that I trust on Twitter or Facebook, I can rely on them to help me process information and to find important online political resources, from news articles to innovative data about politics and government.

On the one hand, then, there are many new ways in which the mass public can leverage online resources, and the information that is accessible to them is highly relevant, more readily available, and personal. On the other hand, this use of online resources suggests the potential for an expanded informational divide between the wired and analog, and between the politically aware and politically disinterested, that affects not only participation in politics but also an average citizen's information about political and policy choices.

If shared identity, political knowledge, and political engagement are the three goalposts for better citizenship, how can new media, with a change in seeking, sharing, and receiving political information, change the quality of citizens' decisions? How can we evaluate whether these changes are affecting only those who are already interested, already engaged, or already informed? In the chapters that follow, we focus on describing the American Internet voter—that is, the American voter who has access to new media. This gives us our population of interest, these are the citizens who have the capacity to take advantage of the new media revolution. We also want to know whether people have equal access, because if not, it dramatically limits the capabilities to have a shared identity.

We then address three critical components of the new media revolution. First, we look at patterns in information seeking. We are particularly interested in the timing of information acquisition as it pertains to elections. We focus on political knowledge acquisition surrounding primary elections. Second, we look at patterns in receiving. Here, we are particularly interested in deliberation that occurs within the online communities. We focus on what is perhaps the lowest-quality deliberative forum: comments posted on YouTube videos. We are interested to describe what kind of community this is. Are people "shouting" at each other? Are they "listening" and responding to each other? Do they post across the political spectrum? We are also interested in the patterns with which political representatives are contacting voters directly, through new media. This direct communication is one of the terrific advantages of the new media revolution and has the potential to increase trust in government. What kinds of communications do we see? Are these communications political? Are they truthful?

Third, what gets shared online? Are people more willing to share memes that are funny, positive, or negative? Do they share political content online more than they do in person? Here we observe that indeed political social norms are surely more likely to be contagious in person, as the online revolution has yet to dominate in-person communication. Online politics plays a role, but standard human friendship and interaction is still dominant.

In the next chapter, we consider who is the average American who engages the political process online and how that has changed in recent years. In particular, we want to address questions about fairness: Do all Americans have access to new media? If access is equal, who is using new media more?

SUGGESTED READINGS

At the close of each chapter we provide a set of readings that could be appropriate for classroom instruction or simply for a deeper look into the debates raised. Here we have focused our attention on three primary texts that debate the role of the Internet in establishing equity in political voice in American democracy.

Sunstein, Cass. 2007. *Republic.com 2.0*. Princeton University Press.

Schlozman, Kay Lehman, Sidney Verba, and Henry E. Brady. 2012. *The Unheavenly Chorus: Unequal Political Voice and the Broken Promise of American Democracy*. Princeton University Press.

Bimber, Bruce A. 2003. *Information and American Democracy*. Cambridge University Press.

CHAPTER 2

The American "Internet" Voter

WHO IS HOWARD DEAN?

Just seven months after his inauguration in January 1991, Vermont Governor Richard A. Snelling died of a heart attack. A little-known part-time doctor and part-time lieutenant governor named Howard Dean filled the governor's office. A decade later, armed with a campaign focused on universal healthcare and fiscal responsibility but minimal national recognition, Dean entered the presidential contest. Surprisingly, by autumn of 2003 Dean was the frontrunner for the Democratic nomination for president. Leading up to the Iowa caucus, he held a strong plurality in the polls and shattered previous fundraising records. Dean won the endorsements of Al Gore and the AFL-CIO (the National Union Umbrella Organization). Dean's 2004 presidential bid ended with defeats to candidates John Edwards and John Kerry in the early caucuses and primaries and a now infamous media gaffe "scream" speech.[1] That Dean's presidential campaign was unsuccessful is not surprising. He was a political unknown who was unlikely to appeal to his party's base. So, how do scholars explain his brief but remarkable success?

The summary explanation for Dean's success is that he moved his campaign operations online. He organized supporters using social networking websites like meetup.org and used the Internet to collect campaign contributions online. The Internet allowed him to create more effective "back-end" operations—fundraising and coordinating volunteers; his campaign did not use the Internet as much for "direct sales" (i.e., political advertising). In thinking about this campaign, we need to consider whether Howard Dean's success could have been possible without new media. Who could he mobilize and why were these strategies effective?

In short, the Dean campaign established a community that had online access, was politically engaged, and participated in the social media of the day, which included blogs and chat rooms. (Remember, 2004 is pre-Twitter, pre-Facebook, pre-smartphones.) These three components allowed supporters to transcend geographic boundaries. Howard Dean's campaign relied on a connected public. His core supporters were already online and used the Internet for political engagement. His supporters already knew how to share information through social media. Thus the campaign, relying on this community, connected supporters more quickly and with greater social visibility than ever before, organizing without geographic constraints. Such a strategy also had spillover effects on the unconnected. When Dean supporters organized a meetup, being online was not a requirement for attending the event. Online Dean supporters could tell their offline friends about it and bring them along. Likewise, the mainstream media could learn about the ideas and positions of the Dean campaign through the blogs and social media activities of Dean supporters, which provided yet another mechanism of spreading the campaign's message.

Dean's campaign strategy innovations have subsequently been followed by other political entrepreneurs in the United States and internationally. Comparatively inexpensive information technology, coupled with a core of devoted supporters, can be leveraged to a political underdog's advantage in campaigns. The new media revolution lowered the resource barriers for political engagement.

The benefit of these lowered resource barriers is not felt by everyone. There exist two dramatic divisions in the use of new media to engage with politics. The first division is in terms of persistent inequalities in society. At the time of the Dean campaign, the digital divide was quite acute but, fortunately for the Dean campaign, the liberal activist population who supported his ideals were also likely to be active with new media. Yet digital differences exist and persist across the socioeconomic spectrum. Access to new media is decidedly unequal, and moreover, the patterns of access follow existing social cleavages in American society based on race, age, education, income, and gender. Much has already been written about the persistence of a digital divide in terms of access to information technology (Norris 2001). The focus of this research has been on a digital divide based on economics and user skills. In general many of these differences have decreased as the cost of access has decreased. That is, while there remains a division based on socioeconomics and demographics, this division has gotten smaller and less concerning over time.

The second division is substantively more alarming, as it deals more directly with representative politics. That is, there are different patterns in use between those who are politically engaged and those who are politically indifferent. On average, new technology has not led to higher aggregate levels of political engagement—this benefit is transferred only to a select group of citizens (Prior 2005). In *Voice and Equality*, Sidney Verba, Kay Lehman Schlozman and Henry Brady (1995) argue that differences in political resources result in systematic distortion in the perceived preferences of the public. More recently, Brady et al. (2013) have found that this systematic distortion has continued into the new media world. It is important to remember that, when thinking about new media, there are very real differences in the degree to which citizens engage with politics using technology. These differences reflect two intertwined issues. First, some people just care about politics more than others. These political junkies watch Sunday morning news shows with a latte in one hand and their phone in the other, tweeting and reading tweets about the various shows. Most people, though, are not this political. Second, even among people who care about politics, some just know how to use technology and new media to communicate with politicians or government leaders and effect change.[2]

That nontraditional candidates like Dean can enter the national political stage and affect the political dialogue benefits democratic politics in the sense that it gives citizens more choices. It implies that information technology establishes a different kind of political community. This community is not limited by geographic boundaries and can enable a greater flow of information from citizen to citizen. Yet, this community is also limited to only those citizens who have access and interest. Democracy is threatened both by inequalities associated with political engagement and by inequalities in socioeconomics. Information technology fails some citizens by giving disproportionate voice to others.

In this chapter we explore digital differences in terms of new media use. We focus on three specific questions (listed below). In order to evaluate whether candidates like Howard Dean are able to systematically produce a new kind of political community, we focus on establishing a series of facts about the average American voter and his or her political engagement online. We want to know if there are divisions in terms of access to new media. We also want to know whether there are divisions in terms of political interest and political use within the population of new media users. Then, finally, we want to know if the community of political new media users change as a consequence of being politically engaged online. In particular, we ask:

1. Are there systematic demographic or socioeconomic differences in who has access to new media? Shared patterns of access are critical to establishing a shared identity.
2. Are there systematic differences in who engages with politics online? Are there systematic patterns in who uses new media for political purposes?
3. Are there changes in political knowledge as a consequence of lower costs of information and distribution?

DIGITAL CITIZENS: NEW MEDIA ACCESS

In April 2014, The *Colorado Independent* reported the following story:

> Last week the [Colorado State] House GOP caucus blew up twitter when its more conservative members called an impromptu caucus to try to replace Minority Whip Kevin Priola of Henderson with Rep. Polly Lawrence of Littleton. While their caucus chair, Littleton Rep. Kathleen Conti, found that effort out of order because the Whip position wasn't vacant, things will certainly progress now that Priola has officially announced his resignation.[3]

From this story, you would expect that this local political story from Colorado was national news—after all, it blew up Twitter!—but it wasn't. In fact, a search of

Google News shows that there were just a handful of news posts from Colorado media sources about the story. The story may have been important for a small portion of the Colorado political scene and, for the reporter who wrote the story, her Twitter feed might have had many different Tweets related to this issue. However, this political intrigue in Colorado "blew up" just one small of the world of Twitter.[4] For people who were in this Twitter network, the number of tweets may have made this small bit of intrigue seem quite important, when actually this was an issue being discussed in an isolated discussion bubble. It is quite possible that only a few Twitter users were discussing this issue.

If you are reading this book, you are likely to come to the subject with certain biases in your mind about the Internet and politics. You experience politics in a specific way, based on your friends, your social networks, and your digital networks. As political scientists, we both experience politics in a very specific way. We use Facebook and Twitter and, on these networks, we are friends with or follow many other academics, reporters, and politicians. Many people experience some level of politics daily on social media during the month or two prior to a presidential election but have very little political exposure outside of campaign season. As political scientists, we experience high levels of political content on social media all the time, such as on a random Saturday in February. Similarly, people who work in the media experience politics in very unique ways. Most of their colleagues—their work friends—are using social media constantly. They are highly connected to others across social media and are great users of these networks in their jobs and, as with many people, their work life bleeds over into their personal lives. If you follow media types on Twitter, they can seem to be online constantly.

Why is this important? Because all of us use what psychologists refer to as a "representativeness heuristic" when we consider things like how many people are using the Internet and the manner in which they use it. For example, if you use Twitter all the time to follow politics and all of your friends use Twitter all of the time to follow politics, you might assume that everyone uses Twitter all of the time to follow politics. The idea that people use Twitter only to follow Kim Kardashian, professional wrestlers, or *The Walking Dead* would not come to your mind.

This issue is well illustrated by the so-called Facebook or Twitter revolution that occurred in Egypt in 2011. In February 2011, the month that Egyptian President Mubarak stepped down, there were 5.2 million Facebook users (11% of the adult population) in all of Egypt. As Pippa Norris (2012) noted, the idea that the Arab Spring was a Facebook or Twitter revolution is belied by the fact that Middle Eastern countries are highly bifurcated, both economically and online. Elites in Arab Spring countries may have been online, and the communications across elite networks were important at various stages to informing the media about what was going on in these revolutions. However, the mass public in Arab countries was not on Facebook or Twitter talking about the revolution. The mass public was using more traditional networks of communication. These communications may or may not have been enhanced by elites communicating messages from social media to this mass public via speeches, conversations, text messages, or posters. Because Western elites were reading the tweets and posts of Egyptian elites during the Arab Spring, they attributed greater significance to Facebook and Twitter than was probably warranted.

When we consider the digital citizen in the US context, we try to avoid the representative heuristic problems and focus on what data tell us about how people use the Internet and the limits to how we can interpret these data. We do not assume that everyone who is on Twitter follows politics or the news, or that every Twitter user is tweeting and reading tweets every day. What we do is present the online adult and then consider how this person uses the Internet to participate in politics. To do that, we need to look at systematic patterns in data. In particular, we need to focus on data that is not collected online.

The Offline Adults

The best data on Internet use in the United States is the Pew Internet and American Life Projects surveys that have been conducted by the Pew Research Center for more than a decade. This project has documented the penetration of Internet use in the American public since May 2000. We plot the data from May 2000 to May 2016 for the percentage of American adults who report using the Internet or email, at least occasionally, in Figure 2.1.

The figure starkly illustrates the dramatic change that has happened over the last 20 years: in May 2000, there were more offline Americans than online Americans. Quite quickly that role reversed, and indeed by 2017 barely 15% of Americans are offline. Before we take a closer look at what is happening online in terms of politics, let's take a look at who is offline. It will be important to consider this issue, as these are individuals who do not have access to the tools of the new media revolution and are not directly influenced by exposure to new media. Who are they?

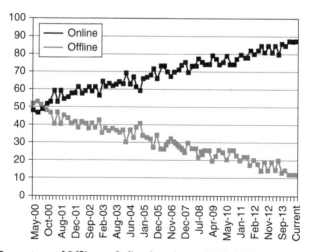

Figure 2.1 Percentage of Offline vs Online Americans, 2000–2017
SOURCE: Pew Research Center

Fortunately the Pew survey lets us take a closer look at these offline adults. The Pew survey also gives us some additional insights into the particular points and types of access. Not every survey question is asked every year. In the figures and results in this chapter, we present data from 2000 to 2016. Whenever possible we have included the most recent survey item's results, as Internet and new media use patterns have changed rapidly in an age of decreasing costs and increasingly ubiquitous access.

In spring 2013, Pew conducted one of their annual surveys examining the public's use of the Internet, which provide the basis for much of the analysis contained here. In April 2013, 85% of adults reported that they use the Internet at least occasionally. So who are the adults who are offline? We know that Internet usage is not uniform. Certain demographic groups are much more likely to use the Internet compared to others, and these gaps between users and non-users of the Internet are typically referred to as digital divides. Age, income, and education are typically considered strong predictors of Internet use, and in Figure 2.2, we see these factors being highly predictive in the United States. This figure plots

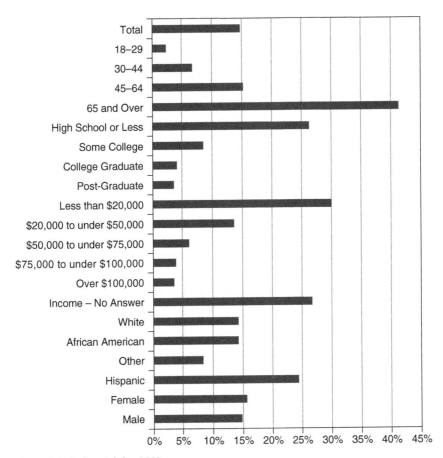

Figure 2.2 Online Adults, 2013

SOURCE: Pew Research Center

the percentage of Americans who are offline by demographic group [or category]. The length of the horizontal bar describes the percentage of people in that group [or category] who are offline. So, for example, if we focus on the second row of data, we see that less than 5% of American adults age 18–29 are offline. If we focus on the fifth row of data, we see that more than 40% of American adults age 65 and older are offline. It is these discrepancies that we want to be particularly attuned to in this chapter.

This summary provides our first opportunity to consider who may be systematically excluded from an online political community of new media users. When we consider the age of people not online, we see that 15% of people aged 18 and older are not online. This is a relatively small proportion of the American public. However, if we look more carefully into the composition of that 15%, the differences between the young and old are pronounced. Only 2% of respondents aged 18 to 29 fail to use the Internet at least occasionally, but 41% of those aged 65 and older are offline adults. Similarly, 26% of people with a high school diploma or less in education are offline, compared to just 4% of college graduates. Across the income spectrum, 30% of individuals who have an income less than $20,000 are not online, but only 4% of those earning $75,000 or more are offline. We also see divides in the United States across racial and ethnic groups; 14% of white, non-Hispanics and 14% of African American adults are not online, compared to 24% of Hispanic respondents.

These patterns have been remarkably consistent in the last several years. In the spring of 2016 Pew conducted another annual survey examining the public's use of the Internet. As of April 2016, we again observe that age, education, income and race produce a digital divide. We plot the updated data in Figure 2.3.

For the typical reader of this book, the proportion of the American population that does not have use the Internet at least occasionally is likely to seem remarkably high: 17.37% (weighted). That is, one out of five Americans don't use the Internet, at least occasionally. These are citizens who are not reading the newspaper online, they aren't checking the news on Facebook, who aren't getting Twitter updates, and who aren't being pummeled with emails from candidates asking them to donate time or money to campaigns. These are people who are outside the mainstream of new media. Consistently these are people who fall along canonical divides in American political life: of those who have incomes less than $20,000, 36.86% do not use the Internet, at least occasionally. Compare this to those who have incomes over $100,000. Only 2.73% of those individuals report being offline.

We would guess, based on Figure 2.2, that age is the strongest predictor of being offline and that education and income follow close behind. We can do a simple analysis to determine which factor most strongly predicts not being online.[5] In order to consider all of these factors together, let us imagine a hypothetical person who is a white male aged 30 to 49, has a college degree, and has an income between $50,000 and $75,000. There is a 93% chance that this person uses

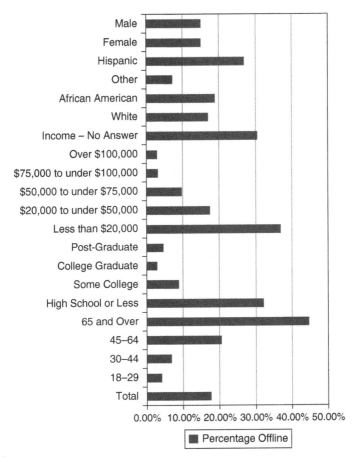

Figure 2.3 Offline Adults, 2016
SOURCE: Pew Research Center

the Internet, at least occasionally. Now, we can change various attributes of our person and consider how they affect his likelihood of being online.

- What if we change this person's age and make him 65 years old or older? Now, he is 33 percentage points less likely to be online compared to when he is aged 30 to 49. (If we make him 18–29, he is 6 percentage points more likely to be online compared to the 30- to 49-year-old).
- If we change his education to having a high school diploma or less, he is now 11 percentage points less likely to be online.
- If we lower his income to less than $20,000, he is now 22 percentage points less likely to be online.
- If we change his ethnicity to Hispanic, he is now 7 percentage points less likely to be online.
- If we change his gender to female, she is now 3 percentage points less likely to be online.

All of the changes we made can be added up to give us an entirely new person. In the examples above, our hypothetical baseline person (white, male, aged 30 to 49, college degree, and an income between $50,000 and $75,000) became a Hispanic female, aged 65 years old or older, with high school degree or less, and an income less than $20,000. Our new person's likelihood of being offline equals the sum of our baseline (93%) and the changes we made to age (−33 percentage points), education (−11), income (−22), ethnicity (−7), and gender (−3). The likelihood that this new person is online is only 3%! So age most strongly predicts a person being online, with income and education both having very strong effects on being online as well.

So one key question we should consider is whether the likelihood of various key demographic groups engaging in political activities online has changed over time. Fortunately, we can use a series of surveys—the American National Election Study (ANES) in 2000 and 2004 and the Pew Internet and American Life Project surveys from 2006, 2008, 2010, and 2016—to see how the online political activities of various demographic groups have changed over time. Using these surveys, we see that, over the last decade, there have been dramatic changes in how the Internet is used for political purposes. These nationally representative surveys allow us to look at which characteristics most closely predict an association with being politically active online. Consistent with our previous analysis, we are particularly interested in which socioeconomic and demographic groups have Internet access. We are particularly keen to know whether these patterns have changed over time. We present the results of our analysis in Figure 2.4.

Figure 2.4 is relatively simple to interpret. The vertical (y) axis represents the percent probability that there is a difference in the outcome variable—here, whether the respondent has Internet access—between the two demographics being compared. We examine differences in online access between (1) men and women, (2) people aged 9 and 97, (3) nonwhites and whites, (4) people with a grade school education and people with an advanced degree; and (5) Democrats, Independents, and Republicans. Each symbol (triangle or circle) represents the estimated difference between the two demographics. If the number is positive, then the demographic noted at the top of the graph is more likely to be online and if it is negative, then the opposite is true. The dashed line represents zero, so symbols closer to zero have a smaller effect and symbols that are further away from zero have a larger effect. For example, for the comparison between men and women, we see that, in 2000 men are slightly more likely than women to be online, by about 2%. In 2016 this effect has reversed, so that women are slightly more likely to be online. One thing to note about these coefficients is that they are extremely small; there are almost no substantive differences in this plot regarding differences in access. It is also important to note that these differences are observable holding all else constant in terms of age, race, education, and party identification.

The graphs for age, race, and education all show minimal changes from 2000 to 2016. From a normative perspective, these changes have been positive as the differences between groups have generally converged toward zero or else exhibited no meaningful trend. In 2000, each year of age decreased the probability that

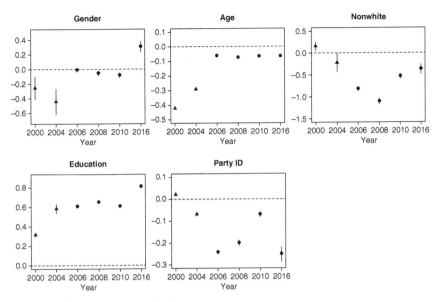

Figure 2.4 Variables that Predict Internet Access
The vertical (y) axis represents the percent probability. Triangles denote coefficients estimated from the American National Election Study while dots denote coefficients estimated from the PEW Internet and American Life Study. The horizontal dotted line is at zero. Solid vertical lines represent 95% confidence intervals. Symbols that are further away from the dotted line represented larger effects and symbols whose solid lines overlap the dotted line are not statistically distinguishable from zero.
SOURCE: Pew Research Center, American National Election Study (ANES)

someone was online by almost half a percentage point (.4%). That is, people aged 20 were 20 percentage points more likely to engage online compared to those aged 70. By 2008, those differences had largely disappeared. Likewise, nonwhites were approximately a percentage point less likely to be online in 2008 but these differences are much smaller in 2016. Educational differences have changed in an interesting way, with each educational achievement associated with just over half a percentage point. We classify education achievements on a seven-point scale, ranging from having a grade school education or less to having an advanced degree. This means that moving from our lowest level of education to our highest level of education would be associated with about a 5 percentage point increase in the probability of being online. When we compare Democrats and Republicans, we see that, from 2000 to 2008, the people who affiliated with either party were, generally speaking, equally likely to be online. In 2010, the year of a strong Tea Party and Republican surge, we see the interesting result of Democrats being online more than Republicans. This suggests that aggregate levels of online activity do not necessarily translate into success at the ballot box. The party identification difference returns to its previous levels in 2016.

Overall, across this figure, we note that the trends are generally positive. More and more people are online, closing the digital divide. The digital divide

Table 2.1 Where Do You Get MOST of Your News about National and International-Issues?

	FAMILY, FRIENDS	TV	RADIO	NEWSPAPERS	MAGAZINES	INTERNET	OTHER
No	65.420	25.060	54.420	58.540	82.160	26.060	96.510
Yes	34.580	74.940	45.580	41.460	17.840	73.940	3.490

Source: The American Panel Survey (TAPS)

persists, but it is less divisive than it was a decade earlier. Much of this book will focus on the American population that is online. By focusing on the online voices we do not intend to negate the very real importance of these offline voices as well. Indeed, in the closing chapters of this manuscript, we return to analyzing the value of online versus offline conversation. We plot one important set of numbers from the American Panel Survey (TAPS), a nationally representative panel survey of American adults. In early 2016, TAPS asked respondents: Where do you get MOST of your news about national and international issues? We plot the results in Table 2.1. Note here that respondents can choose more than one category. Nearly 74% of American adults report gathering news from the Internet, and this number is very similar to the percentage of American adults who report gathering news from TV (75%). These are larger percentages than newspapers or magazines. Remarkably, only 34.5% of respondents say they get most of their news from family and friends. Online information acquisition merits more careful study.

Online America is, demographically, the flipside of offline America. Certain subpopulations have Internet use rates exceeding 90%: people under age 45 (especially ages 18–29), people with some college experience, with bachelors or with graduate degrees, and people earning $50,000 or more. As we would expect, people who are of higher socioeconomic status are online more than are other adults (Verba et al. 1995). Thus it is important to remember that our population of interest already represents a somewhat rarified voice in the American public.

Online Access Points

When you go online, how do you get political information? Using TAPS, a nationally representative online panel survey of approximately 2,000 adult Americans, we asked people in early 2016:

Which of the following is your most common source of news from the Internet? One of the components of the new media revolution has been the dramatic shift in points of online access. With the Internet, no one needs to read political news. Indeed, it would be possible to consume only YouTube music videos, or YouTube videos about cats, or for citizens to spend entire days reading Reddit streams of jokes. So how, then, do people actually *use* this Internet access? Let's take a look. Each type of access is listed followed by the (weighted) percentage of Americans who reporting using this source for news.

Remarkably, as we plot in Table 2.2, the average citizen is using the Internet to gather news from pretty conventional sources. Between TV news websites,

Table 2.2 How Citizens Access News Online

A website of a TV news organization (CNN, Fox, CBS, etc.)	23.28
An internet portal website (Google, AOL, etc.) that gathers news from many sources	30.30
A website of a newspaper	10.72
A website of a radio news organization	2.00
A website of an online news organization (Huffington Post, Politico, etc.)	10.18
A website that specializes in a particular news topic like health or politics	5.09
A foreign language news site	0.85
A blogger	0.46
A group on a social networking site like Facebook	11.33
Twitter updates from a journalistic news source	2.54
Twitter updates from a non-journalistic news source	0.69
I don't read internet news	2.00
Refused	0.54

Source: The American Panel Survey (TAPS)

a general search, radio, online news organizations, and newspapers, we have accounted for almost 77% of all news sources. There is one surprising finding in this table, though. Just over 11% of Americans report *their most common source of news* is a social networking site, like Facebook. This is where the new media revolution is different from previous media shifts. The new media revolution isn't only about reducing the costs of accessing information by providing on-demand content that is available in each person's living room, at their convenience. The new media revolution has to do with how people receive this information, and to a large extent, that shift comes from the fact that information is now frequently shared through an online user community.

Social Media Communities

Let's use the TAPS data to better understand how people use these social media communities to learn about politics. Within our population of online Americans, we want to know how frequently people log in to social media sites. We plot the results in Table 2.2. The volume of Facebook use stands in stark contrast to all other social media sites. Over half of adult online Americans report using Facebook on a daily basis. Given that over 11% of Americans report using this as their most common source of news, online sharing on Facebook starts to play a significant role in how Americans form political opinions and attitudes.

Once we know these are the places where people are active, we can then ask more specifically about the levels of political activity in social media. We tabulate this in Table 2.4. While almost 20% of respondents report following a candidate on Facebook, we see very little other evidence that people are specifically seeking out political information that they could get elsewhere—such as the candidate's website, or other traditional media sites—via social media sites. What, then, are people doing online on these social media sites?

Table 2.3 Social Media Use

	FACE BOOK	TWITTER	WORD PRESS	BLOGGER	TUMBLR	MYSPACE	GOOGLE PLUS
Daily	50.540	5.520	0.780	4.350	1.010	0.230	3.890
A few times a week	20.840	5.680	1.940	4.510	1.940	0.470	5.750
A few times a month	12.990	7.230	2.640	5.830	2.410	1.090	7.310
A few times a year	6.530	8.400	4.040	4.430	3.580	3.890	7.540
Never	7.850	71	87.950	77.990	87.090	91.290	71.070
Don't know	0.860	1.710	2.260	2.570	2.880	2.100	3.810
Refused	0.390	0.470	0.390	0.310	1.090	0.930	0.620

Source: The American Panel Survey (TAPS)

Table 2.4 Political Activity in Social Media

	FOLLOW A CANDIDATE ON TWITTER	FOLLOW A CANDIDATE ON FACEBOOK	FOLLOW POLITICAL SITE ON TWITTER	FOLLOW POLITICAL SITE ON FACEBOOK
Yes	7.740	20.370	6.440	18.580
No	90.870	78.480	91.770	80.520
Refused	1.390	1.140	1.790	0.900

Source: The American Panel Survey (TAPS)

We argue that people are online to exchange information with peers. Here, in Table 2.4, we document the use of these platforms to post, comment, or share political news/content. The results here are pretty astounding in terms of thinking about a new media revolution. The first row describes the individuals who said "yes" to the column item. Over 16% of individuals report they belong to an explicitly political social network group, over 19% report that they have used a social networking site to share political links or articles, over 33% say they have used email to share political links or articles, over 21% report they have used a social networking site to explicitly share their own political opinion, and almost 30% report they have used their email to send their own political opinion to their personal network. This is a tremendous volume of online sharing.

In a recent survey wave, TAPS respondents were asked, "During the past year, have you sent a message via social media (e.g., Twitter, Facebook) about a political candidate or cause?" A total of 31.55% of all respondents said yes. Looking at patterns of access points and use, it appears that the access point that has generated the greatest change has been the opportunity to talk to peers. Understanding not only who has online access then, but also what they are doing with it, will be critical to understand whether this online sharing has the capacity to build better citizens.

Table 2.5 Use of Platforms to Post, Comment or Share Political News/Content

	BELONG TO A POLITICAL SOCIAL NETWORK GROUP	USE SOCIAL NETWORKS TO SHARE POLITICAL LINKS OR ARTICLES	USE EMAIL TO SHARE POLITICAL LINKS OR ARTICLES	USE SOCIAL NETWORKS TO POST OWN POLITICAL OPINIONS	USE EMAIL TO SEND OWN POLITICAL OPINIONS
Yes	16.690	19.510	33.180	21.480	29.300
No	80.160	78.060	64.320	76.410	68.270
Don't know	2.370	1.510	1.310	1.380	1.640
Refused	0.790	0.920	1.180	0.720	0.790

Source: The American Panel Survey (TAPS)

The Cell Phone Revolution

Another surprising aspect of this revolution is the ubiquity of cellular phones. Most college students have never used a rotary phone. Indeed, many college students' only experienced being offline as young children; a coming-of-age experience was buying their first "smart" phone. As Bruce Bimber (2003) has noted, it is hard to study the Internet over time because the Internet is constantly changing and evolving. Today, being online means something quite different than it did just 10 or 15 years ago. In the early days of the Internet, people connected using dial-up services, such as AOL. This was followed by the advent of high-speed, broadband Internet, typically available through cable services and telephone providers. In 2000, 34% of adults had dial-up Internet service and only 3% of adults had broadband service. By 2005, broadband Internet usage exceeded dial-up usage, and by 2013, only 3% of households used dial-up Internet service.

The biggest change in Internet service, however, has been the advent of ubiquitous wireless Internet. Wireless Internet use would be a significant innovation itself, but it is even more so because of the growing ubiquity of "smartphones," cell phones with full Internet browsing capabilities. Smart phone penetration has exploded in the United States over the past several years. If we just compare the years 2011 with 2013, we see that smartphone penetration among adults went from 37% in 2011 to 56% in 2013.[6] These numbers are relatively amazing when you remember that the iPhone was only introduced into the adult market in 2007 and was only available on multiple cellular telephone carriers beginning in 2011. Today, just slightly more adults have Android phones compared to iPhones.

Wireless Internet is especially important because it can lower the cost of Internet access for many people. Given that 91% of adults have cell phones and 36% of households are cell phone–only households, it is often very cost-effective for a person to add a wireless data plan to their phone compared to buying broadband Internet services and a laptop or tablet computer.[7] The Pew Internet and Adult Life surveys have found that 9% of adults use the Internet but have no home Internet access, and cost is the most common reason given for not having home Internet.

Let's compare the American online population to the American population that uses their cell phones to access the Internet. We plot the American online population's demographics in Figure 2.5. The Pew surveys ask whether a person accesses the Internet mostly from home or mostly from their cell phone. In April 2013, 34% of adults were mostly accessing the Internet from their cell. In Figure 2.6, we show the way in which members of each demographic group with Internet access primarily accessed the Internet. Again, the length of the black bar describes the percentage of that row category that accessed the Internet primarily via their cell phone. We see that cellphone Internet users are more likely to be Hispanic or African American adults, are aged 18 to 29, have only a high school degree, and earn less than $50,000 per year. Individuals who are wealthy (incomes over $100,000 per year), have college degrees or post-graduate education, are white, and are aged 45 or older are more likely than average to access the Internet using a computer or tablet device and thus are less likely to access the Internet using their cell phone.

Just as we did before to consider what attributes make a person more or less likely to primarily access the Internet, we can repeat this process to evaluate what attributes make them more or less likely to access the Internet from their smart phone, assuming that they use the Internet at least occasionally. We can again imagine our hypothetical person who is white, male, aged 30 to 49, has a college

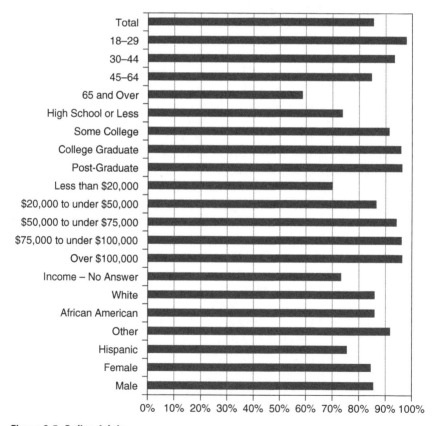

Figure 2.5 Online Adults
SOURCE: Pew Research Center

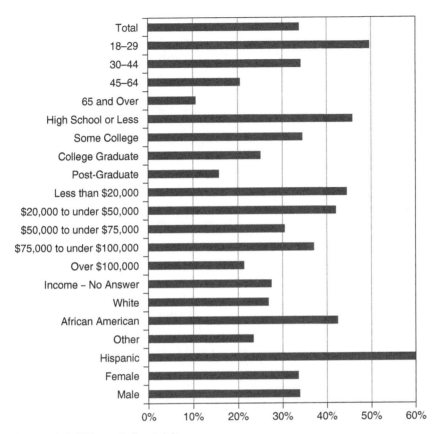

Figure 2.6 Cell Phone Online Adults
SOURCE: Pew Research Center

degree, and an income between $50,000 and $75,000. There is a 26% chance that this person primarily accesses the Internet from his phone. We can again change various attributes of our hypothetical person and consider how they affect his likelihood of being online.

- If we make him 18–29, he is now 10 percentage points more likely to get online mostly on his smartphone.
- If we change his education to having a high school diploma or less, he is now 13 percentage points more likely primarily to use a smartphone to access the Internet.
- If we lower his income to between $20,000 and $50,000, he is now 8 percentage points more likely to access the Internet primarily via his phone.
- If we change his ethnicity to Hispanic, he is now 26 percentage points more likely to access the Internet mainly via cellphone.

As we did before, we can see how different our new person—a Hispanic male, 18 to 29 years old, with high school degree or less, and an income less than

$20,000, who is online is from our hypothetical baseline person (white, male, aged 30 to 49, college degree, and an income between $50,000 and $75,000, who is online). Our new person's likelihood of primarily accessing the Internet with his phone equals the sum of our baseline (26%) and the changes we made to age (+10 percentage points), education (+13), income (+8), and ethnicity (+26). The likelihood that this person primarily accesses the Internet from his phone is 83%. Here, we see that ethnicity most strongly predicts a person accessing the Internet primarily via their phone, with education, age, and income all having very strong effects as well. The availability of smartphones has revolutionized Internet access for minority and low-income Americans. In the past, personal Internet access meant having a personal computer and then an Internet service provider. Today, Internet access represents the marginal costs related to getting a slightly more costly phone (compared to a basic cell/text-only phone) and purchasing a data plan for the phone.

Social Internet Adults

When we note how different the Internet of today is with the Internet of 2000 or 2004, one of the biggest differences is the social nature of the Internet. In the early years of Internet use, social media consisted of chat rooms, email among users, and game downloading contained in what were referred to as bulletin board systems (BBSs), where a person dialed into a specific computer service via a dial-up modem. With the advent of AOL and Yahoo!, the social aspects contained within narrow BBSs could be accessed through the portals that these companies developed. However, as we noted previously, with most people accessing the Internet via dial-up service—and then at home via dial-up services—social interactions online for the first decade of the Internet (1995–2005) tended to revolve around one-on-one communications via a chat system or a small chat room exchange with people who might or might not be actual friends.

Social media has been defined by websites such as MySpace, LinkedIn (both launched in 2003), Flickr (launched in 2004), Twitter (launched in 2006), Facebook (launched to public in 2006), Tumblr (launched in 2007), Instagram (launched 2010), and Google+ (launched 2011). The explosion in use of social media has corresponded with the rise of smartphones, tablets, and wireless computing. With the ability to take photos with a phone and then upload them, social media can support visual, audio, and text media, enhanced by the geographic positioning system (GPS) incorporated into all smartphones. We can share what we are doing, where we are, and what we see there, all with a couple of clicks on a smart phone.

We are interested in examining who uses social media for any purpose before we consider who uses social media to communicate political messages. We again use the Pew Internet and Adult Life 2013 survey data to address this question. In Figure 2.7, two sets of percentages speak to Twitter use. First, we show the percentage of adults 18 years old or older answered "yes" when asked if they use the Internet to use Twitter. Second, we show the percentage of all adults

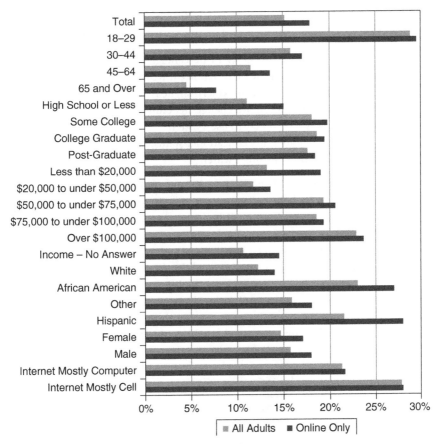

Figure 2.7 Online Social Adults – Twitter

SOURCE: Pew Research Center

who use Twitter, where we include the offline adults in the denominator (the offline were not asked this question, since it was not relevant to them).

Some of the numbers here might surprise you at first. For example, Hispanic and African American adult respondents who are online are twice as likely to use Twitter compared to white online respondents. Keep in mind though that the median Hispanic person in the US in 2010 was 27 years old and the median African American adult person was 32, which are 15 and 10 years younger, respectively, compared to the median white person in the United States in 2010 (42 years old).[8] As we see in Figure 2.7, younger people (18 to 29) are twice times as likely to use Twitter compared to older adults (45 and older). We also see that the respondents who have attended even some college are more likely to tweet than those who have a high school degree or less. There is also a relatively large difference—6 percentage points—in Twitter use between mostly cell phone Internet people and those who mostly access the Internet via a computer.

Changing the characteristics of our hypothetical baseline person (white, male aged 30 to 49, college degree, and an income between $50,000 and $75,000, who is online) will let us see whether certain different subpopulations are using Twitter. There is a 22% chance that our hypothetical person uses Twitter.

- If we make him 18 to 29, he is 14 percentage points more likely to use Twitter. (There is no significant difference if we make him older than 45).
- If we change his race to African American, he is 15 percentage points more likely to use Twitter and if we change his ethnicity to Hispanic, he is 13 percentage points more likely to use Twitter.
- If we change his gender, his educational status, or his income, it does not change his likelihood of using Twitter.

So here, we can see that if he is 18 to 29 years old and African American, there is a 51% probability he uses Twitter and if he is an 18 to 29 years old there is a 49% probability he uses Twitter. If he is younger and white, there is a 36% probability he uses Twitter, a 29% (25%) lower use rate compared to our younger African American (Hispanic) person.

Figure 2.8 shows the percentage of adults (online and all adults) who answered "yes" when asked if they ever use the Internet to use a social networking site like Facebook, LinkedIn, or Google+. Here, we see that there are relatively interesting differences between the responses for online adults and for all adults. When we consider all adults, we see that white and Hispanic respondents are equally likely to use social media. We also see that there is a large gap between

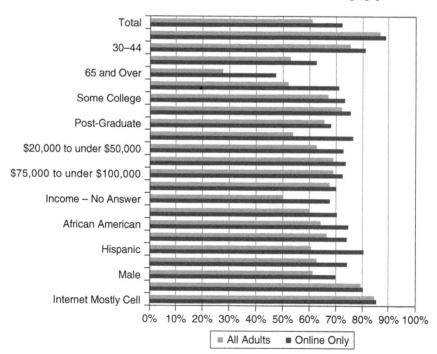

Figure 2.8 Online Social Adults – Social Network Sites
SOURCE: Pew Research Center

those who make under $20,000 annually and those who make more than $20,000 as well as for those who have a high school degree or less and those who have at least some college education. Remember that offline Americans are more likely to be lower income, less well educated, and members of minority populations.

However, once online, we see that Hispanics are the most likely to use social networks, using them 10 percentage points more than whites (the baseline category). Online African Americans are also more likely to use social networks compared to whites who are online. People who primarily use their cell phones to access the Internet use social media more than those who primarily use their computers. We also see that age is a strong predictor of social media use.

So let's see what happens when we change the characteristics of our hypothetical baseline person (white, male, aged 30 to 49, college degree, and an income between $50,000 and $75,000, who is online). There is an 83% chance that this person uses social media. There are only two factors that change the likelihood that a person will use social media. First, if this person is 18 to 29, he is 10 percentage points more likely to use social media but if he is 45 to 64, he is 10 percentage points less likely to do so. If we change his gender from male to female, he is 5 percentage points less likely to use social media.

The primary concern with respect to the "digital divide" had to do with differences in access to online content. While we do see systematic differences in access, these differences are much smaller than they were a decade ago. Access, it seems, has become much closer to universal as the costs of technology have decreased and it is increasingly possible to rely on phone technology to provide a point of entry. We are additionally encouraged about access to social media. Race and ethnicity, for example, do not predict the same kind of disparate social network access between Hispanics, African Americans, and whites that we would have historically anticipated. The concern about inequality, then, has now shifted, as while more citizens have access to new media it is not clear whether access will eliminate differences in use for explicitly political purposes. If some segments of the population are using new media to consume information about sports while others are consuming information about politics, for example, then the voices of some voters may be heard more loudly than others by political representatives.

DIGITAL DIFFERENCES: NEW MEDIA USE BY THE POLITICAL AMERICAN

Now that we know what our online universe looks like, we can turn to an examination of how online Americans used the Internet for political purposes in the 2012 election. Here, we use data from the Pew Internet and American Life Project's 2012 Civic Engagement Survey. This survey was conducted in August 2012 and asked a variety of questions about online and offline political activities. We begin by examining a basic question: how many people are using the Internet to follow news and politics and how often do people talk about politics online, compared to offline discussions.

In the top half of Table 2.6, we show the percentage of adults who used the Internet to get news or look for political information in 2012, as well as the percentage who used social media and used Twitter. We provide the percentages for all adults, including offline adults, and then for only online adults. We see that online news use is quite high in 2012. Two-thirds of all adults and 78% of online adults used the Internet to get news and more than half of all adults and almost 60% of online adults used the Internet to search for political or campaign information in 2012. Online news reading is more prevalent than social networking use and most people are not getting news via Twitter. If we think back to the anecdote we relayed about Twitter and the Colorado newswoman, this is an incredibly important fact to establish. For active Twitter users, or even active social media users, it may seem incredible that so few individuals report getting news via these channels. This point emphasizes the critical need to establish facts about the American Internet voter via survey data. To understand the impact of new media we need to understand the profile of the average user.

In the bottom half of Table 2.6, we show the frequency by which people discuss politics across various online and offline modes. For the online modes, we only report responses for those individuals who use the Internet at least occasionally. We see that most people discuss politics through traditional offline modes—face-to-face or via telephone—and online adults talk about politics online much less frequently. Roughly 70% of online adults responded that they

Table 2.6 Use of the Internet for Political News and Discussions, 2012

	ALL ADULTS			ONLY ONLINE	
	NO	YES	OFFLINE	NO	YES
Get news online	18.9	66.6	14.6	22.1	77.9
Look online for news or information about politics or the 2012 campaigns	35.2	50.2	14.7	41.2	58.8
Use a social networking site like Facebook, LinkedIn or Google Plus	26.3	59.1	14.6	30.8	69.2
Use Twitter	71.4	13.9	14.6	83.7	16.3

	DAILY	WEEKLY	MONTHLY	LESS THAN MONTHLY	NEVER
How often do you discuss politics and public affairs with others in person, by phone call, or by letter?	14.6	27.1	19.7	15.1	23.5
How often do you discuss politics and public affairs with others online – such as by e-mail, on a social networking site or by text message?	5.4	12.8	12.1	13.6	56.0

Source: Pew Research Center

never or very rarely (less than monthly) talk about politics via email, social networking sites, or text message. It appears that individuals are still mostly likely to engage about politics in a social capacity offline. This coincides with what we believe to be true about online social engagement more generally, which is that it mirrors offline engagement. For example, people who are friends on Facebook are generally unlikely to decide to "like" the same bands. But, if two individuals are tagged in a picture together, the probability they "like" the same band dramatically increases (Christakis and Fowler 2009). The same is true with respect to political behaviors that are socially contagious: People are more likely to mirror the behavior of another if they are tagged in pictures together on Facebook (Bond et al. 2012), if they share a household (Sinclair, McConnell, and Green 2012), if they share a neighborhood (Sinclair, McConnell, and Michelson 2013), and in general if they have a common social component that allows them to establish a political conversation (Sinclair 2012). The patterns of online political use begin to parallel what we expect for the American Internet voter. We expect individuals to gain information online—for example, to read the news online—but to have political conversations with others in person.

Communication with others via social media is one way that people can be engaged in politics online. There are two others to consider. The first is how people are contacted by campaigns or other political organizations. People can be contacted in a variety of ways to be involved in political or interest group activities from working for a candidate to going to a meeting, to giving money to a cause. Table 2.7 shows the percentage of American adults who were contacted, using various online and offline modes, to engage in political or interest group activities. Each question shows the responses only for individuals who stated that they have access to that media. For example, the texting question was only asked of people who said that they text and the Twitter question was asked only of those who use Twitter.

We see some very interesting findings here. First, text messaging is clearly the mode of contact that individuals and groups use least frequently to contact people asking for them to engage in collective action activities. Second, letters remain a common technique for asking people to engage in collective actions. Direct mail was the original way in which groups contacted individuals

Table 2.7 How People were Contacted in 2012 for Collective Action

	DAILY	EVERY FEW DAYS	WEEKLY	LESS THAN WEEKLY	NO
Receive email asking you	5.8	6.5	9.3	15.0	63.4
Receive a phone call asking you	1.7	3.7	6.5	23.1	64.9
Receive a letter in the mail asking you	1.4	3.8	7.3	30.7	56.9
Receive a text message asking you	0.4	1.2	1.3	3.8	93.3
Get asked in person	0.2	1.1	2.2	19.2	77.3
Get asked on a social networking site	2.7	3.8	6.8	13.1	73.6
Get asked on Twitter	1.1	0.4	5.7	7.7	85.0

Source: Pew Research Center

asking for money for people to engage in direction action. The interesting comparison here is between contacting via phone, letter, and email. Clearly, we can see that there is a slight bias toward contacting via letter versus phone or email. However, email contacting is done much more frequently than either telephone or letter. This makes clear economic sense; the incremental cost of sending an additional email is almost zero, whereas the cost of sending an additional letter, even at bulk, pre-sort rates, is over $0.30. Email is also less intrusive than a telephone call and less costly as well, given the infrastructure costs associated with telephone banks. Social networking has a cost structure similar to email, and we see that the daily and every-few-day contacting rates using social media are slightly higher than telephone or letter contacting. Interest groups and campaigns clearly were starting to use social media more in 2012, but this usage had not caught up with the use of email, which groups likely had much more experience using. One caveat with this data, of course, is that this is what people remember. It may be that an even larger portion of individuals, for example, received a letter in the mail asking them to participate but that some number of survey respondents simply forgot they had received such a letter or failed to open it. That these patterns display what respondents recall and believe to be true is a limitation of this kind of data collection. Yet it does appear that campaigns are systematically focusing on more traditional kinds of communication strategies.

The second way that people engage in politics online is when they reach out directly to government, campaigns, or other political organizations. We evaluate this in Table 2.8. Here we look at the patterns in use for all survey respondents and then specifically focus on those who have online access as well. For each specific activity in this table, we see the rate at which respondents report that they have engaged in that particular activity in the final column of the table.

When we look at how people have participated in politics, we see in Table 2.8 that, in most cases, people are more likely to have engaged in an offline activity than an online one. For example, more people have contacted a government official in a traditional method compared to an online one. In some cases, it may be that people think that the traditional activity will be more effective. For example, signing a petition online may seem rather pointless if the government will not accept an electronic signature as an official signature on the petition. People are more likely to comment on news stories online compared to through traditional media.[9] Given the efforts of the media to make online commenting easy, we should not be surprised that people comment online more than via writing a letter. This kind of political participation was not possible prior to the establishment of online politics and is the kind of engagement that we suspect can be transformational for the American Internet voter. A full 21% of our online sample reports commenting on an online news story or blog post. This pattern is further supported in other data. A significant number of online individuals are engaging in political actions that are only (easily) possible online: posting pictures or videos relating to a political or social issue (almost 11%) and sending text messages about a political or social issue (almost 18%).

Table 2.8 Political and Collective Actions – Online vs. Offline

WHO ASKED	ACTIVITY	NO	YES
All	Contacted a national, state or local government official in person, by phone call or by letter about an issue that is important to you	78.6	21.4
Online Only	Contacted a national, state or local government official ONLINE, by email or by text message about an issue that is important to you	80.0	20.0
All	Signed a paper petition	77.7	22.3
Online Only	Signed a petition ONLINE	80.1	19.9
All	Sent a "letter to the editor" by regular mail to a newspaper or magazine	96.6	3.4
Online Only	Sent a "letter to the editor" to a newspaper or magazine ONLINE, by email or by text message	95.4	4.6
All	Called into a live radio or TV show to express an opinion	93.3	6.7
Online Only	Commented on an online news story or blog post to express an opinion about a political or social issue	78.7	21.3
Online Only	Posted PICTURES or VIDEO online related to a political or social issue	89.1	10.9
Online Only	Sent text messages to others about a political or social issue	82.4	17.6

Source: Pew Research Center

It is not the case, though, that everyone is taking advantage of these opportunities. In Figure 2.9 we see that, even among people who are online, most individuals do not engage in online political action. Only 20% of people who use social networks (e.g., Facebook or Google+) or Twitter follow politicians on social media. Approximately one-third of people use social networks or Twitter to post political stories, post their own thoughts on political or social issues, encourage people to take action on issues of importance to them, repost or retweet stories, or like political or social issues that others have posted. Just over one-third of people have used social media to encourage people to vote.

One theory about online political engagement was that when the costs decreased there would be an enormous increase in the levels of political participation and in particular in political deliberation. If the costs, it was theorized, were reduced to where more voters could participate without succumbing to social pressure and the restrictions of time, and had access to a plethora of information, there would be a flurry of direct communication between representatives and voters, and among voters. We do see some of that kind of engagement in Figure 2.9, but it is clearly not the case that every citizen wanted to participate in online politics. People are most likely to "like" a political issue and least likely to follow an elected official on social media. That is, people are not becoming this idealized citizen as a consequence of new media.

So over time, who has become an online political person? Here we again turn to older surveys from the ANES and the PEW Internet and American Life

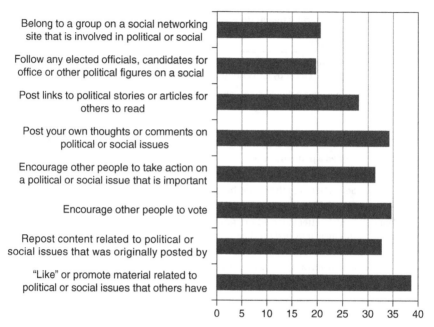

Figure 2.9 Online Political Activities

SOURCE: Pew Research Center

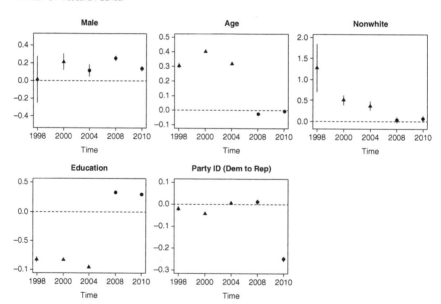

Figure 2.10 Variables that Predict Political Internet Use

The vertical (y) axis represents the percent probability. Triangles denote coefficients estimated from the American National Election Study while dogs denote coefficients estimated from the PEW Internet and American Life Study. The horizontal dotted line is at zero. Solid vertical lines represent 95% confidence intervals. Symbols that are further away from the dotted line represented larger effects and symbols whose solid lines overlap the dotted line are not statistically distinguishable from zero.

SOURCE: Pew Research Center, American National Election Study (ANES)

project, focusing on the key predictors that we anticipate will be problematic for representation (gender, age, race, education, and party identification). We use a survey question that asks respondents if they search about politics or campaigns online.

As before, we focus on those coefficients (the triangles and dots) that are further away from the dotted line at zero. The vertical lines that cross through those symbols represent a measurement of uncertainty. We are particularly interested in the trends that we can observe from these coefficients. We find that there have been real decreases in differences in political use in terms of race, age, and education. That is, for each of the comparisons (white vs. nonwhite, for example), the differences in political Internet use have decreased over time. The effect of gender has been fairly stable. Up until 2010, there was no difference in use based on party identification. In 2010, we see a dramatic increase of Democratic respondents reporting that they had searched about politics or campaigns online. These coefficients are again largely encouraging. While political Internet use is clearly not universal, differences are decreasing over time.

The Online Political Person

Now let's compare three different types of people: the person who reads news online, the person who follows politics online, and the person who uses social media to encourage people to take collective actions online. As we did before, we can start by considering our hypothetical baseline person (a white male, aged 30 to 49, with college degree, an income between $50,000 and $75,000, who is online, and is a political independent) and then see what happens when we change the attributes of this person. In Table 2.9, we present comparisons between those who seek out news online with people who seek out political information online and between those who use social networks and those who use social networks to encourage actions and encourage voting.

The first thing of note is that there are many more people who are reading the news online or who are using social media who are not looking for political news or engaging in political activities online. There are three key findings here. First, being partisan matters. If you clearly identify as being a Democrat or a Republican, you are more likely to engage in online political activities. For many people, politics is like a sport and, as such, they follow politics and participate as they can, just like people who follow sports do (Abramowitz 2012). Second, younger people are more into online media and online politics, as would be expected. They use social media to communicate, and, for many young people, that includes communicating about political and social issues of interest to them. Finally, we see that education matters, at least when we compared those with only a high school degree or less with those who have some college or more. Those who have a high school degree or less are much less likely to engage in political activities online or follow politics online compared to their peers who attended at least some college.

Table 2.9 Online Actors

	ONLINE NEWS	ONLINE POLITICS	SOCIAL NETWORK	SOCIAL NETWORK – ENCOURAGE ACTION	SOCIAL NETWORK – ENCOURAGE VOTE
Baseline	79.4	59.8	67.5	30.2	34.3
Age 18–29	N.S.	8.6	25.1	8.9	N.S.
Age 45–65	−12.2	N.S.	−18.1	N.S.	N.S.
Age 65 and Older	−21.0	−10.4	−37.2	N.S.	N.S.
HS or Less	−20.6	−27.4	−7.3	−13.9	−10.4
Some College	−4.9	−11.0	N.S.	N.S.	N.S.
Post Graduate	N.S.	N.S.	N.S.	N.S.	N.S.
African American	N.S.	N.S.	N.S.	N.S.	N.S.
Other Race	N.S.	N.S.	N.S.	N.S.	N.S.
Hispanic	N.S.	N.S.	N.S.	N.S.	N.S.
Income Under $20,000	−15.9	−17.4	N.S.	N.S.	N.S.
Income $20,000–$50,000	−8.7	−8.7	N.S.	N.S.	N.S.
Income $75,000–$100,000	−3.2	N.S.	N.S.	N.S.	N.S.
Income Over $100,000	N.S.	N.S.	N.S.	N.S.	N.S.
Income No Response	−16.7	−14.7	−14.1	N.S.	N.S.
Male	N.S.	N.S.	−15.7	−6.4	N.S.
Republican	N.S.	7.1	N.S.	7.9	8.3
Democrat	N.S.	6.7	N.S.	7.7	9.8

N.S. – Difference not significant from baseline.

Source: Pew Research Center

Looking across the range of reported political activities, we note that furthermore people remain more likely to participate in traditional politics. Political conversations with others offline dominate political conversations online with others. People were most frequently asked to participate in politics via letters in the mail. People were most likely to sign a paper petition. Nonetheless, there are large fractions of people who are now participating in politics via nontraditional means. Over 18% of our survey respondents report that at least weekly they discuss politics online (via email, social networking site, or text message). Over 35% of our respondents report they are solicited to participate in politics via email. Most interestingly, there is a rising opportunity to participate in a new way—over 21% of those respondents who are online report they had taken the opportunity to comment about an online news story or blog post. There are systematic differences in who engages with online politics or uses new media for political purposes, but these differences are shrinking as at the same time there are rising opportunities to engage online.

ENGAGING THE POLITICALLY DISINTERESTED

To summarize our results so far: There are systematic differences in access as well as systematic differences in the use of new media. We are particularly concerned about these differences insofar as they allow people to acquire political information, as we observe high levels of offline political engagement focused on the social component of politics—offline social political conversation, for example, dominates online social political conversation. Fortunately the differences in access and use are small, but they are persistent and follow historical cleavages in American society. One question to consider is the following: Suppose everyone was automatically given Internet access. Would that eliminate these inequalities? Would all voters be equally well informed and have similar levels of political knowledge?

One way to know what the effect is of the Internet would be to do an experiment, giving free Internet to people who did not have Internet access already and then measuring the effect of the Internet on their levels of political knowledge. Fortunately, we are able to do something very similar: we are able to study a group of people who are new Internet users, looking at the extent to which their political knowledge changes over the course of two years. Early in 2011, TAPS launched a multiyear panel survey designed to solicit the opinions of a nationally representative sample of American adults.[10] The survey polls respondents monthly using an online platform, so in order to generate a nationally representative sample it was necessary to provide those respondents who previously did not have Internet access with free Internet access. As both these respondents (those who are provided Internet access) and the remaining respondents then reply to a series of survey items on political interest, knowledge, and participation, we can then evaluate whether the primary cause of disparity in online political activity is attributable to differences in access (here, remedied). It is important for our inferences that we are able to compare those who are new-to-Internet to those who already had Internet over this period of time, so that we can infer that changes in political knowledge are associated with Internet access and not salient political events, for example.

The American Panel Survey (TAPS) is publicly available (free!) data. TAPS is a nationally representative panel survey that conducts an online poll of up to 2,000 adult respondents monthly. The survey was started in December of 2011 and administered by Knowledge Networks (now GfK Knowledge Networks) for the Weidenbaum Center at Washington University. The sampling frame used to select the 2,000 respondents is the US Postal Service's computerized delivery sequence file (CDSF), which covers around 97% of the physical addresses in all fifty states including P.O. boxes and rural route addresses. This frame is appended with information regarding household residents' names, demographic characteristics of the inhabitants, and landline telephone numbers obtained from other sources such as the US Census files and commercial data bases

(Continued)

(e.g., White pages). The respondents are recruited based on a random stratified sample, where Hispanics and young adults between 18 and 24 years of age are slightly oversampled in order to account for their tendency to under-respond to surveys. Through the support of the Weidenbaum Center, those individuals without Internet access are provided with a computer and Internet access. (More technical information about the survey is available at http://taps.wustl.edu.) At the beginning of each month, members of the panel receive a notification to complete the new survey. Each wave remains open for approximately one month and takes between 15 and 25 minutes to complete. Such breadth of data provides researchers with a unique opportunity to investigate trends and changes at the individual level. For example, if an individual remains active in the panel for two years, TAPS collects over 1,000 variables at 24 different points in time for one individual. Such design invites investigation of individual-level change over both the short and long term.

We investigate a respondent's reported level of political knowledge (measured by asking ten factual questions to see how many respondents can get correctly). We consider what the effect is from the first to the last time the respondent replied (from January 2012 to May 2013). This gives us the longest possible temporal distance between questions, so ideally the effects of the Internet should be largest in this calculation.

In terms of political knowledge, the average respondent who already had Internet access was able to answer 4.88 of the political knowledge questions correctly (1,224 total respondents) in January of 2012 while the average respondent who did not have Internet access was able to answer 3.75 of the political knowledge questions correctly (95 total respondents). This difference is big—1.13 questions—and is statistically significant, which means that we can distinguish this difference from zero using traditional measurements of statistical uncertainty (95% confidence intervals). The online public is more politically knowledgeable. The question, then, is whether the online public is more politically engaged because they have greater resources (education, income) on average or whether simply having access to online political content can transform a respondent to becoming a more politically knowledgeable group of citizens. Our core question, then, is whether the difference between those respondents who did and did not have Internet access at the start of the survey will be eliminated after a period of time, as those who did not have access have now one barrier to obtaining political information eliminated. Interestingly, when we return to these respondents in May of 2013, both groups are better equipped to answer the political knowledge questions. The average respondent who did have prior Internet access answers 5.56 of the political knowledge questions (934 respondents) while the average respondent who was granted Internet access answers 4.90 of the political knowledge questions (41 respondents). One possibility for this increase is that these respondents have all been participating, monthly, in a political survey. Note here that both groups increase their levels of political knowledge. Yet the difference between these increases—since both groups have been participating in the survey but only one was granted new Internet—is the key quantity to focus on. The difference between these new values is 0.66 questions (just over half of a question); while the group who had prior Internet access is still more politically knowledgeable, the size of that difference has shrunk. That is, while the respondents who are new to Internet access still have lower measureable levels of political knowledge, they now appear to be more similar to the respondents who are prior users of the Internet. What we will do next is to formalize this statement a bit by quantifying the increase in political knowledge for the two groups.

The main quantity of interest for us, then, is the difference between the two increases. That is, if we focus on the difference *between* those differences— the difference in the increases themselves—those individuals who are granted Internet access do in fact exhibit a larger increase in their political knowledge. The group given Internet access answers more questions correctly as a consequence of receiving access: that is, they improve more in terms of their political knowledge over this two-year time horizon than the group that already had Internet access, in the order of magnitude of about half a question.[11] Individuals who are granted access to appear to become more politically knowledgeable when barriers to access are eliminated. Over our 1-year study, they don't quite catch up to the group that already had access, but they get pretty close.

This result puts the trends that we have seen in Figure 2.4 and Figure 2.10 into a broader context. Over the last decade both Internet access and the use of the Internet for political purposes has become increasingly universal. Given that we are able to evaluate the impact of political knowledge as a consequence of Internet access, we then have concrete evidence for the normative importance of closing that gap. We also begin to establish what kind of citizenship is possible with online political activity: a more informed citizenry, better equipped in terms of basic political knowledge.

WHO IS BERNIE SANDERS?

We opened this chapter describing the fundraising success of a nontraditional presidential candidate. We maintained that Howard Dean's campaign strategy innovations have subsequently been followed by other political entrepreneurs in the United States and internationally. We maintained that comparatively inexpensive information technology, coupled with a core of devoted supporters, can be leveraged to a political underdog's advantage in campaigns. Who, exactly, has benefited from the lowered resource barriers for political engagement, created by the new media revolution? Here we give you a single illustration from the 2016 presidential primary campaign to argue that indeed the new media revolution allows candidates who would otherwise have been marginalized to enter mainstream politics: Senator Bernie Sanders.

Like Dean, Senator Sanders hails from Vermont. Unlike Dean, Sanders had a history of success winning higher office (he has served in the US Senate since

2007). But like the Dean story, when Sanders announced his presidential campaign in April 2015, he was seen as an unlikely winner. He insisted on grassroots financial support: at the end of a year of campaigning, the campaign had raised a total of $73 million from more than 1 million people making 2.5 million donations, with an average donation of $27.16.[12] He rejected large donations from corporations, any donations from the financial industry, and any donations from a Super PAC associated with the financial industry. In what was quite a surprise to most pundits, Sanders won 23 primaries and caucuses and approximately 43% of pledged delegates to Clinton's 55%. It seems exceptionally unlikely that Sanders—who was not a "household" name ahead of the election—could have been successful without the support he garnered via new media. Indeed, throughout his campaign, although Sanders was able to solicit rally attendance greater than Clinton's, he received significantly less free media. For example, according to *Democracy Now*, as of December 2015 the three major networks—CBS, NBC, and ABC—had spent 234 minutes reporting on Trump and 10 minutes on Sanders, despite their similar polling results.[13] In the brave new world of new media, candidates like Senator Sanders can run serious national campaigns.

DESCRIBING THE AMERICAN INTERNET VOTER

We opened this chapter with an anecdote about presidential candidate Howard Dean and his campaign from 2004. Dean was able to use new media and link it with traditional face-to-face meetings to revolutionize how community building was done in campaigns. The anecdotes about the Dean campaign, and new media in general, claim that new media allows political entrepreneurs like Howard Dean to activate "high demanders" of digital participation and then use these people to communicate with the rest of the public. We closed this chapter with an illustration for how the type of candidate who can be successful with new media has consistently changed, and argued that Bernie Sanders illustrates our point for 2016. Since much of the literature on this topic has focused on anecdotes, and in particular the narrative has focused exclusively on those who are already online, our plan in this chapter has been to ascertain something about these "high demanders." To do this, we want to build our knowledge as to who, in general, is online and engaged in politics.

Our aim in this chapter has been to establish a series of basic facts about the American Internet voter. We want to know whether there are systematic demographic or socioeconomic differences in who has access to new media, who engages with politics online, and who uses new media for a political purpose. To be able to answer these questions we have turned to surveys, conducted by phone, to establish a profile of the average American Internet voter. We find significant reason to believe this person is mostly representative of the American public. While there are some small divisions in terms of the digital divide in terms of socioeconomics and demographics, we find that access is more universal than ever before. Only 15% of Americans are offline. Older Americans are less likely to be online, lower income categories are less likely to be online, and lower educational categories are less likely to be online. While African Americans and Hispanics are more likely to be offline than Whites, there are relatively minor differences in terms of gender. Encouragingly Hispanics and African Americans are more likely to be engaged in social media online, perhaps offsetting some portion of the impact of the difference in online access.

In terms of who participates in online politics, we find that the average person is more likely to participate in traditional offline politics. Political conversations with others offline dominate political conversations online with others. People were most frequently asked to participate in politics via letters in the mail. People were most likely to sign a paper petition. Nonetheless, there is a large fraction of people who are now participating in politics via nontraditional means. Over 18% of our survey respondents report that at least weekly they discuss politics online (via email, social networking site, or text message). Over 35% of our respondents report they are solicited to participate in politics via email. Most interestingly, there is a rising opportunity to participate in a new way—over 21% of those respondents who are online report they had taken the opportunity to comment about an online news story or blog post. There are systematic differences in who engages with online politics or uses new media for political purposes, but these differences are shrinking as at the same time there are rising opportunities to engage online. Moving forward in this book we evaluate the extent to which people participate in online politics and continue to compare this to their offline participation.

The survey data show us that the "high demander" digital community is linked to age (younger people are online more) and education and income. One key question to consider is whether smartphones and other technologies will change the education and income cleavages. We are encouraged by the use of new media for political purposes by nonwhites. We do see evidence that those individuals who are now coming online will become more politically knowledgeable over time.

We are particularly interested in evaluating whether citizens are in fact changed by their political participation online, via new media. We are able to use a novel dataset to evaluate the extent to which having Internet access causes people to become more politically knowledgeable over time. We look at individuals who do and do not have Internet access and ask them a series of questions about their political knowledge. Then, we give free Internet access to those respondents who did not have access. After 18 months, we ask everyone—both those who did and didn't have access before our intervention—the same set of political knowledge questions. We find that individuals who did not have access before our intervention have benefited from access and can answer more of the political knowledge questions than they could beforehand, controlling for the increase in knowledge for those whose access was constant.

These findings speak directly to the impact of new media in terms of establishing a shared identity and a more politically informed citizenry. With the digital divide falling, we are encouraged that not only is an increasingly diverse population present online but additionally a more diverse population is politically engaged online. Furthermore, in the span of our Internet-access study, we see that those individuals who are granted Internet access are quickly able to procure political knowledge. We hope this would imply they could also make similar-quality political choices. The Internet-access study also speaks directly to a question very difficult for us to measure: whether new media improves the quality of citizenship. We seldom have data on users both before and after they have engaged with new media. In this brief snapshot, we are able to discern the improvement in political knowledge that comes from having Internet access. Internet access does not only benefit the already politically informed citizen.

We continue to see great changes occurring in the Internet environment. Work from the Pew Research Center has found that older Americans are quickly catching up with younger Americans in their adoption of technology. Smartphone adoption has increased almost fourfold over the last five years among those aged 65 and older. Two-thirds of those aged 65 and older use the Internet regularly today; only 40% used the Internet regularly just 7 years ago. Only one-third of older Americans use social media today, but in 2008 only 2% used any sort of social media.[14] One of the biggest remaining cleavages in the United States is between those who live in urban areas compared to those in rural areas. Compared to all adults in the United States, rural adults are 10 percentage points less likely to have access to broadband internet, 10 percentage points less likely to have a smartphone, and eight percentage points less likely to have either a tablet or a desktop or a laptop computer.

There is another component to having the majority of voters with an online presence. Joe Trippi, in his book on Howard Dean's campaign, wrote that "we had misnamed this era *The Information Age*" and that it should instead be called "*The Empowerment Age*," where "the Internet is the most democratizing innovation we've ever seen—more so than even the printing press. There has never been a technology this fast, this expansive, with the ability to connect this many people from around the world. If Madison was right, and the people can only govern when they can "arm themselves with the power which knowledge gives," then the Internet is the first technology that truly gives people full access to that knowledge—and empowers them with the ability to do something with it. (Trippi 2008, 235–236). With 85% of the American public online, and with online access so clearly improving political knowledge, it is hard not to get excited about the possibilities of the new media revolution in politics. This revolution gives citizens real power and voice. This chapter shows that a large percentage of Americans have access to new media, although there are key populations that are less likely to be online. The introduction of smartphones has played an important role in allowing lower-income Americans to have access to the Internet and become key participants in the world of new media. It is important to note that access to new media occurs alongside access to other media; never have there been so many outlets for news, with radio and television and print media outlets existing alongside new media. Having established a series of facts about what an average user and a high-demand user look like in terms of survey data, we now turn to a series of specific questions about what kind of political exchange happens via new media. We are particularly interested in extending our understanding of how and when an average Internet voter becomes informed about politics. We want to expand our understanding of political knowledge to see when citizens rely on Internet access to make political decisions.

SUGGESTED READINGS

Trippi, Joe. 2008. *The Revolution Will Not Be Televised*. Harper.

Cohen, Cathy. 2010. *Democracy Remixed: Black Youth and the Future of American Politics*. Oxford University Press.

Leighley, Jan E., and Jonathan Nagler. 2014. *Who Votes Now? Demographics, Issues, Inequality and Turnout in the United States*. Princeton University Press.

CHAPTER 3

Googling Political Information

As we noted in the Preface, most of the time citizens have little need to stay on top of the day-to-day movements related to politics. Day-to-day we do not need high levels of political information. For people who are political junkies this is an anathema; the political junkie cares about the moment-by-moment development of any political issue. Knowing the "tick-tock" of how a political situation developed is exciting, and listening to Sunday morning news analysis shows is as exciting to the political junkie as the NFL pregame shows and football analysis shows, like ESPN'S *NFL Countdown*, are to a football fan.[1] People obsessed with politics and news often assume everyone else is too—a form of the "false consensus effect"—and also do not understand how people who are not following politics moment by moment can make decisions without an encyclopedia of information.[2]

FOLLOWING FOOTBALL, FOLLOWING POLITICS

In this chapter, we focus on presidential primary elections and discuss how the Internet can facilitate being an active citizen in these primaries. But before we do, let's keep using the football analogy for a moment. If you are a huge professional football fan, you probably watch all the football analysis shows, the games of the week, and even pay for specialized football news on websites for people like you. You know which wide receivers are probable to start next week, what the quarterback rating is for every starter in the league, and who is up and down. Week in and week out, you know what is going on across the league. But a lot of football fans only really watch or follow one or two teams, and the most watched game of the year is the game at the end: the Super Bowl. This makes sense. The Super Bowl is *the game* that matters. Whoever won or lost Week 6 of the season does not matter. What matters is the Super Bowl.

What is true in football is also true for elections. If you are a political junkie, following politics moment by moment may be exciting. Thinking about the 2016 presidential election, knowing which campaign consultants are in or out with Governor Jeb Bush or Senator Hillary Clinton can be exciting for the junkie. Knowing which campaign is raising money (or not) can be exciting. But for most people, what matters is the Super Bowl, the November general election, and the playoffs, the presidential primary. What most people do not realize is that, before the primary elections, there is an *invisible primary*, where the party elites—the big donors, prominent interest groups, and others who shape each political party's agenda and ideology—are working to winnow the field so that *their* preferred candidate is likely to win the general election.[3]

In the context of elections, being an active citizen all the time can be difficult and not overly helpful. Instead, people need to be active citizens at certain politically salient moments. The month or two before a primary election—when political parties choose their nominee for an office—is one time when individuals need sufficient political information to be able to cast a vote. Primary elections require citizens to be active because they pose a relatively unique problem for voters: they cannot rely on party labels to help them choose among candidates. In almost all primary elections, the candidates are of the same party.[4] Instead, an individual needs to acquire enough information about each of the candidates and weigh how each candidate's platform accords with their own personal preferences in order to cast a "correct" primary ballot.

Primary elections are also a time when a voter may want to vote *strategically*—to cast a vote that will have the most impact, even if it is not a vote for their first-choice candidate. Strategic voting, which is also referred to sometimes as sophisticated voting, requires a person to identify likely trends in public support for each candidate so that they can ensure that their vote is not wasted on a candidate who is likely to lose (Abramson et al., 1992). For example, in the 2012 election, imagine you really liked Representative Ron Paul (a libertarian with a conservative bent); in the primary election you could just vote for him. However, Representative Paul was not likely to win the Republican nomination. In order to maximize your vote impact, you might decide to vote strategically to help the candidate you viewed as being the second-best candidate. So, if you hated the frontrunner Mitt Romney—who had a reputation as not being a "true conservative" because of his policies and positions during his time as governor of Massachusetts—and thought Newt Gingrich or Rick Santorum would be a better choice than Romney and had a better chance of beating him, you might vote strategically for Gingrich and not vote for your first choice (Ron Paul). Citizens need to accumulate this political knowledge ahead of key political moments.

And how does the public accumulate this knowledge? Much of this knowledge is not gathered online. For some time, scholars have argued that the Internet is a tool and information resource that could revolutionize politics.[5] It has definitely changed how politicians campaign. For a campaign, creating an Internet presence is a low-cost and necessary affair; it is the modern campaign office and a digital yard sign all rolled into one. Almost all candidates, even for local offices, create campaign websites, engage in online fundraising, blog, email citizens, and broadcast their campaign activities on the Internet. Because this content has been created, the Internet makes it relatively inexpensive for individuals to engage in information search for the races and referenda/amendments/questions that are on their ballot. Voters can use the Internet to examine a candidate's campaign platform and determine whether the candidate is a person who had fulfilled previous promises or has reneged in the past.[6] As we showed in the previous chapter, a relatively large percentage of Americans go online to engage in political activities. Consider that, in 2012, 66% of social media users (39% of American adults) had engaged in some civic or political activities with social media. This helps to frame the broader literature about how those who are online report searching for political information.[7]

The standard way to measure political knowledge is to use answers to factual questions. For example, a researcher might give survey respondents the names of public officials and ask what office they hold. While knowing these political facts is surely different from having the right information to cast a correct vote in an election, researchers have long assumed that answering political factual questions correctly is associated with having enough civic and political knowledge to cast a correct vote. Recently this measurement strategy has come under attack, as there are some concerns about noise in the measurement strategy—for example, survey respondents have varying propensities to guess factual political questions correctly (Mondak 2001) and there are sometimes arbitrary coding decisions about correct and incorrect survey answers for open-ended questions (Gibson and Caldeira 2009; DeBell 2013). Most critically, however, knowing political facts simply does not incorporate all components of an actual political decision (Gilens 2001; Lupia 2006; Abrajano 2015; Barbaras et al. 2014). One of the problems with assuming that knowing political facts equals knowing political knowledge is it relies on an estimate of political knowledge that is fully divorced from the political context in which the voter is making an actual decision. For example, suppose there is a person who has a terrific knowledge base of political facts. Yet in their Republican primary election, that same voter cannot just find out the party of the candidate or look at the endorsements each candidate received to know how to vote. Every candidate is going to be a Republican, they are all likely to claim to be a "real conservative," and all are going to have been endorsed by some prominent conservative. This means that, in order to figure out whom to vote for, the voter has to actually do a bit of digging in the context of this specific election. It is a pretty big assumption to assume that knowledge of political facts would enable this voter to cast a correct vote, because it assumes that because the voter is knowledgeable that they will then bear the burden of acquiring new political knowledge. We want to challenge that assumption, and we want to focus on the *digging* instead of prior evidence of having acquired political knowledge.

For the remainder of the chapter, we focus on that digging. First, we focus on digging for information by voters in the 2008 presidential primary election. As we show, this election was one where knowing all of that political factual knowledge was not likely to help at all in determining which candidate to vote for in

2008. Voters need new information, both about the candidates and about the likely choices of other citizens, so they do not "'waste'" their vote on a noncompetitive candidate. Using data from Google searches, we present evidence that voters are actively seeking out this information. Focusing on the active role that citizens play in seeking information and whether there is empirical evidence that citizens are engaged in that kind of seeking process is a different way to conceptualize evidence that citizens are responsibly bearing the burden of the democratic process. As we show, citizens do often seek political information ahead of primary elections, which is encouraging with respect to their competence in casting a primary vote. It is likely a stronger indicator of their political knowledge than previous measures, as it allows us to understand whether they attempt to become informed about a particular electoral context at a particular political moment. Then, we turn to another instance where voters have terrific need to acquire complicated political information to make a good electoral decision—the California open primary. In both cases, it is critical that voters acquire new political knowledge in order to make good decisions. New media should allow voters access to that knowledge, and this chapter focuses on whether or not there is evidence they seize that opportunity. Furthermore, we are able to then see if there is an association between the acquisition of political information and political engagement—in this case, voting in elections.

POLITICAL FACTS VERSUS POLITICAL KNOWLEDGE

Most eligible voters in America possess low levels of "political knowledge." In surveys, this type of knowledge is typically measured by asking people questions about government structure, government process, and key people in government. For example, people will be asked about political facts, such as to name the position held by John Roberts (Chief Justice of the Supreme Court). Using this measure, many eligible voters are fairly uninformed about politics and some people do not know very basic information about their government, such as the number of US senators who represent their state in Congress. Many eligible voters have difficulty locating themselves and the various candidates on an ideological spectrum, remembering the names of candidates, and knowing where any particular candidate stands on a broad set of issues.[8] More recently, some studies have argued that the Internet may marginally increase access to information that can increase political knowledge.[9] Others studies have found that the Internet has simply provided people with more media choices but this has not increased political knowledge.[10] It is common for people to conceptualize political knowledge as the mere possession of political facts. However, more recent research suggests that knowledge of political facts does not necessarily correspond with real political knowledge, what a voter needs to know in order to make informed voting choices. There are many times when people can make competent voting decisions even if they cannot answer many standard political knowledge questions. Many, if not most, voters are able to make voting decisions based on very simple cues.[11]

We can examine the purported level of political knowledge in the American public using the American National Election Study (ANES), a survey that asks questions about political knowledge. In the ANES 2012 survey's "User Guide and Codebook" there are questions that are specifically designated as political knowledge questions.[12] These data show that most political knowledge questions are difficult for many respondents. For example:

- 62.1% of respondents knew "which party had the most members in the House of Representatives in Washington before the [2012] election";
- 55.2% of respondents knew "which party had the most members in the U.S. Senate before the [2012] election";
- 90% of respondents knew "how many times an individual can be elected President of the United States";
- 78.1% could pick out that Medicare was "a program run by the U.S. federal government to pay for old people's health care" [as opposed to a health program for the poor (16.9%), a private health plan in all 50 states (3.3%), or a nonprofit organization that runs free clinics (0.9%)]; and
- when asked which program the government spends the least—national defense, Medicare, Social Security, and Foreign Aid—only 32.2% correctly answered foreign aid.

Knowing the religious affiliation of each candidate was also classified as a political knowledge question. Respondents were asked, "is President Obama/ Governor Romney Protestant, Catholic, Jewish, Muslim, Mormon, some other religion, or is he not religious?" Just over two-thirds of respondents knew that Governor Romney was a Mormon; only 9% answered Catholic, and 8.6% said "don't know" or refused to answer. For President Obama, questions were much more scattered, with 29.5% choosing Protestant, 23.1% choosing Muslim, 14.1% choosing not religious, and 13.6% answering "don't know" or refusing to answer.

The data from the 2012 ANES show that a larger percentage of Americans fail to correctly answer many of the standard political knowledge questions in surveys. However, it is not clear that the failure to answer these questions correctly truly indicates a limitation on the part of the voter relative to their ability to make quality political decisions. Critics have shown that validity tests of the standard political knowledge battery are mostly flawed and that a person's political knowledge plays little role in their ability to cast correct "votes" in a laboratory environment.[13] This research suggest that political scientists need to consider other ways to evaluate whether or not citizens are getting the political knowledge they need.

THE INTERNET, LEARNING, AND PRIMARY ELECTIONS

So primary elections are an example of a time when voters have to actually hunt for information that will allow them to make an informed voting choice. Given that party labels cannot be used as a cue and even ideological labels may not be helpful, since every candidate may say that they are the "real" liberal or conservative in the race, voters have to dig a bit deeper to select a candidate. An active voter will be searching for this information, and we can find evidence of the importance of the Internet in voter learning if voters are actively seeking out political information online, especially at times in which such information is crucial for informed decision-making. We use data from the 2008 presidential primary election to examine when and how people have used the Internet to search for information to make an informed vote choice.

We already know quite a bit about how voters make candidate choices in primary elections. In general, research shows that voters choose a candidate by picking a candidate with one or more of the following characteristics:[14]

- the candidate most likely to win the nomination,
- the candidate most likely to win the election in November,
- the candidate who most closely reflects the voter's own choices, or
- the candidate who has a personality or sociodemographic characteristic to which the voter is attached.

Voters may need very little information to make this kind of decision, regardless of their decision-making process, and voters can become informed voters based on simple information gleaned from political parties, interest groups, political figures, or other cues.[15] In the context of primary elections, the primary factors that have been found to affect vote choice are candidate qualities, especially descriptive characteristics, such as age, gender, or race.[16] It is not surprising that candidate qualities are important factors in making a vote choice in this context. Robbed of the party cue and of clear issue differentiations (as primary candidates typically hold similar positions), voters look to "softer" factors for clues to the candidate's values. Norrander (1996, 1986b) notes that using candidate qualities is rational for voters because media coverage of political races tends to focus on candidate qualities to the exclusion of coverage of issues. Personal cues are of most importance to voters who are less interested in the campaign. Acquiring political information in a campaign can be costly, and what we do know is that all voters, regardless of partisan affiliation, may have their participatory behavior shifted due to costs of voting (Alvarez, Levin and Sinclair 2012).

Abramson et al. (1992, 55) studied sophisticated [strategic] voting in the 1988 presidential primaries and found that "most voters do support the candidate they most prefer; but many appear to be guided in part by information about the candidates' prospects of winning their party's nomination, or viability." Basically, people want to vote for the candidate that they truly support, but many people also loathe to vote for a loser. They may vote for their second-choice candidate in a primary to avoid having the candidate that they hate win the primary. The cues that a voter needs to choose a primary election candidate—even when voting strategically—can be gleaned from shortcuts that can be found online.

One of the best examples of an election where searching for information was critical was in the 2008 presidential primary elections. In this election, there was a need for primary election voters to search for information, in both the Democratic and Republican primaries. With President George W. Bush having been elected twice, there was not an incumbent candidate in either the Democratic or Republican presidential primaries. Both major political parties had competitive contests for their presidential nomination in 2008. On the Democratic side, two candidates dominated the field: Senators Hillary Clinton and Barack Obama. These two candidates received by far the most media coverage and were perceived going into the early races as the frontrunners. The other candidates—Senator Joe Biden (DE), Senator Chris Dodd (CT), Senator John Edwards (NC), Governor Mike Gravel (AK), Representative Dennis Kucinich (OH), and Governor Bill Richardson (NM)—were never considered real contenders for the nomination. On the Republican side, the race was initially considered much more wide-open. Senator John McCain (AZ) was an early frontrunner, but former governors Mitt Romney (MA) and Mike Huckabee (AR) were also considered quite viable going into the primary elections (and, indeed, Romney won the 2012 nomination). Much like the 2012 Republican primary elections, several other candidates were also considered quite viable at various points in the process, including Senator Fred Thompson (TN), New York City Mayor Rudy Giuliani (NY), and Representative Ron Paul (TX).

Given that both parties have open primaries, one might not initially expect any differences in Internet search activities between Democrats and Republicans. There is no incumbent to choose from and there are several strong candidates in both primary elections. However, on closer inspection, vote choices in both primaries, but especially the Democratic primary, were made easy for many voters. For the Democrats, the 2008 campaign was historical because neither of the two most viable candidates was a white man. Instead, the two contenders were a white woman and an African American man. The descriptive qualities will be important cues for many Democratic Party primary election voters. Specifically, we would expect that (1) African Americans will engage in less Internet search activity and (2) women will engage in less search activity because of the importance of race and gender cues in making a vote choice. The comedian Larry Wilmore explained the importance of these cues humorously on *The Nightly Show*, when he said:

> I voted for Obama because he's black. People always ask me . . . "Do you agree with Obama's policies?" I agree with the policy that he's black. And then they say "Shouldn't you vote based on principle?" And that's correct. And my guiding principle is that, as long as he's still black, he and I agree on principle.[17]

On the Republican side, there were no simple descriptive sociodemographic cues to guide Republican voters; the leading candidates were all white males. However, two of the candidates were well known for distinctive personal qualities. Senator John McCain was strongly tied to his record as a veteran, and Governor Mitt Romney was strongly linked to his religiosity as a member of the Church of Jesus Christ of Latter Day Saints (Mormon). We expect that these personal characteristics will matter for those voters who can make simple cue decisions based on sociodemographics. Specifically, we would expect that (1) individuals who identify as veterans and (2) individuals who identify as Mormon will engage in less online search activity.[18]

The 2008 primary is also a good election to study because of the structure of the primary elections; for both parties the primary election schedule was very compressed and front-loaded. The first caucus (Iowa) and first primary (New Hampshire) were held on January 3, 2008 and January 8, 2008, respectively. During the rest of January, a small number of primaries and caucuses were held. Then, on February 5, "Super Tuesday," more than 20 states held their presidential primary contests, and on February 9, four more elections were held. After February 9, small clusters of primary elections occurred during March and April, with things ending on June 3. This timing allows us to examine the acquisition of information across multiple states over a relatively short period.[19]

The vast amount of political information online allows any citizen the opportunity to seek out political information directly, without waiting for a traditional media outlet or political elites to provide it. We can examine how people search for information about candidates by seeing how people use Google. Google provides public records for the number of searches, broken down by geography, for particular words using the Google Trends application. We examined how people use Google to search for candidate information by collecting data using Google Trends regarding the search volume, by day and by state, for searches that included the terms "McCain," "Romney," "Obama," and "Clinton" for the period December 1, 2007, to August 31, 2008. These data reflect the number of searches conducted in a state on a particular day that queried Google using one of these words. Google normalizes these data so that it reflects the proportion of the search volume from that state. Two states could have the same percentage of searches for Obama with very different search volumes, because the data has been normalized by the total traffic in that state. Google also scales these data from 0 to 100, where 100 represents the peak search interest possible for those terms in that state. This normalization and scaling process allows us to compare searches across states over time.[20]

Google search data is increasingly used to understand public opinion. People frequently lie in surveys, particularly about sensitive topics.

For example, survey data—including Census data—suggest that the population of homosexual men varies widely across states.[21] Not surprisingly, men who live in more gay-friendly states are more likely to report being gay on Facebook or in surveys. People in states like Mississippi, where there might be a stigma to being outwardly gay, report being gay at very low rates. However, using Google search data, researchers find that approximately 5% of individuals search for gay porn images or videos across states, whether they live in California or Mississippi. People in certain states are just more closeted about their sexual identity. Similarly, Google search data can be used to identify places in the United States where racism is most prevalent and where anti-Muslim attitudes (attitudes which strongly correlate to hate crime activity) are most prevalent.[22] Google data on racism can be linked to political outcomes; areas where there were high levels of searches for racist terms were much less likely to vote for Obama in 2008 than would have been expected.[23]

GoogleTrends data is publicly available and fun to search. Trend data has been used by the *New York Times* to report the most popular Thanksgiving side dish recipe in each state, for example, and is increasingly seen as a key predictor of political behaviors and attitudes from different regions of the United States. In a partnership between Twitter, Google, and the Associated Press, the Associated Press produced the AP Election Buzz Tool to track Google "search interest in political terms" focusing on topics associated with the 2016 election, including presidential candidates and political figures, policy issues, and current events. If you would like to take a look, google "AP Buzz Election Tool."

We can examine whether people are looking for political information in a meaningful way by determining whether individuals are more or less likely to search for the four presidential primary candidates' names in advance of the primary election in their state. We focus on states where both presidential party primaries are held concurrently (Table 3.1).[24] In Table 3.1 we list the 41 presidential primaries (40 states and Washington, DC) in our analysis, along with the dates of the elections. Over this period, there are an average of 1.73 normalized searches per day (with a minimum of 0 and a maximum of 29.2). There are frequent instances of Google Trends reporting zero search volume for a particular state on a particular day. This does not mean that there were no searches for these terms on these days but rather that these terms constituted a low enough portion of the search volume in that state on that particular day that the search volume is represented as a zero. Even during the presidential election season, Johnny Depp, Angelina Jolie, Alicia Keys, Taylor Swift, and *American Idol* dominated the Google culture landscape in 2008 more than did politics.

For each state, we observe the search volume in the state over its entire pre-primary period. For many states, we see a similar pattern; there is an increase in searching prior to that state's primary election and then a decrease in search volume following the date of the primary election. The average search volume appears to be highest in the three days prior to each state's primary and on the day of the primary itself.[25] Individuals are less likely to query Google with the presidential candidate names after their state's primary election has taken place; the need for political information is over and they can go back to following sports, celebrity gossip, and their favorite television shows. Importantly, what we see corresponds with the theory that individuals will seek out primary election information online.

Table 3.1 Presidential Primary Election Dates in 2008

PRIMARY DATE	STATE
December 17th	1st CCAP Survey Window Starts, Ends January 3rd
1/3/2008	Iowa
1/8/2008	New Hampshire
1/15/2008	Michigan
January 24th	2nd CCAP Survey Window Starts, Ends February 4th
1/29/2008	Florida
2/5/2008	Alabama
2/5/2008	Alaska
2/5/2008	Arizona
2/5/2008	Arkansas
2/5/2008	California
2/5/2008	Colorado
2/5/2008	Connecticut
2/5/2008	Delaware
2/5/2008	Georgia
2/5/2008	Illinois
2/5/2008	Massachusetts
2/5/2008	Minnesota
2/5/2008	Missouri
2/5/2008	New Jersey
2/5/2008	New York
2/5/2008	North Dakota
2/5/2008	Oklahoma
2/5/2008	Tennessee
2/5/2008	Utah
2/9/2008	Louisiana
2/9/2008	Washington
2/12/2008	DC
2/12/2008	Maryland
2/12/2008	Virginia
2/19/2008	Wisconsin
3/4/2008	Ohio
3/4/2008	Rhode Island
3/4/2008	Texas
3/4/2008	Vermont
3/11/2008	Mississippi
March 31st	3rd CCAP Survey Window Starts, Ends April 4th
4/22/2008	Pennsylvania
5/6/2008	Indiana
5/6/2008	North Carolina
5/13/2008	West Virginia
5/20/2008	Kentucky
5/20/2008	Oregon
6/3/2008	South Dakota

NOTE: States (and DC) where both party primaries occur simultaneously (41 primaries). This excludes 10 states: Hawaii, Idaho, Kansas, Maine, Montana, Nebraska, New Mexico, Nevada, South Carolina, and Wyoming.

Source: Hall and Sinclair, Google

INDIVIDUALS' SEARCHING FOR CANDIDATE
INFORMATION ONLINE

The data from Google Trends allows us to see clear patterns regarding Internet searches about candidates. However, these findings are very general; these are patterns at the aggregate (state) level and do not tell us much about the individuals who are conducting these searches nor their motivations to search. These results also are not sensitive to other changes that are taking place across the country at varying points at time. In order to determine how individuals used the Internet to search for political information in 2008, we review the results of Cooperative Campaign Analysis Project (CCAP) survey. The CCAP was a special survey, what is called a panel survey; a survey where the same respondent is interviewed multiple times during a given time. In the case of the CCAP, the same 20,000 people were surveyed six different times between December 2007 and November 2008.[26] As you will see, the results from the Google Trends analysis is supported by the results from the CCAP survey. There are clear patterns of political information search associated with the timing of presidential primary elections. In our analysis, we will be comparing how respondents answered questions about their Internet search habits across three waves of CCAP surveys: the first (baseline) survey (conducted between December 17, 2007, and January 3, 2008), the second (conducted between January 24, 2008, and February 4, 2008), and the third (conducted between March 31, 2008, and April 4, 2008).

Based on when these three waves of survey data were collected and when each voter's presidential primary election was held, we can categorize respondents into three "windows." The first window consists of respondents in states that completed their presidential primary elections by January 24. If the state completed its presidential primary election between January 24 and March 31, the respondent falls in the second window. The remaining respondents are in the third window; their state's presidential primary took place after March 31.[27] We are focused on survey respondents who are exposed to the pressures associated with needing to search for political information ahead of a primary election. For respondents in the early presidential primary states, we would expect them to search for information and then be more likely return to their normal search activities afterward. For those in the last primary states, we would expect more searching during the period before their primary, and they may search more than those with early primaries, as each primary provides more information to them about their vote choices.[28] In terms of outcomes, we focus on whether respondents report that they have used the Internet to read about politics in the last seven days. This survey question is asked in each of the three waves, which gives us a survey population of 17,138 respondents. In the first wave, 44.9% of respondents said that they had used the Internet to read about politics in the last seven days. In the second and third waves, these numbers are 47.8% and 52.6%, respectively.

We hypothesize that the primary elections will cause the respondent to read about politics to obtain political information. For each of the three time periods we know:

- whether the respondent is using the Internet to read about politics;
- whether or not the respondent is under the pressure to look for information because of their state's presidential primary election and thus the pressure to search for primary election information;
- whether the respondent is a Democrat or Republican; and
- whether the respondent falls into a group where there is a "cue" to help them to vote (i.e., African American or females in the Democratic primaries and veterans or Mormons in the Republican primaries.)

For each wave, there were two groups of respondents: one group was not exposed to the immediate pressures of a presidential primary election and one group did have this pressure. Within each wave, we compare across these two types of individuals. We also see whether the behavior of each individual respondent changed across different points in time and whether their search behaviors were different based on whether or not they were exposed to the pressure of needing information to understand their upcoming presidential primary election. Of course, it is important to remember that, as we consider these survey data, there were national political pressures and events that also were influencing people to go online to search for news across each of the survey waves, regardless of the primary election timing.

When we examine people's search patterns before and after their state's presidential primary election, we find a consistent pattern.[29] Individuals were more likely to use the Internet to read about politics in the pre-primary window. Specifically, when an individual was exposed to the pressures of having a presidential primary election, they were approximately 3 to 4 percentage points more likely to report they had used the Internet to read about politics in past last week. This effect was true as we compare individuals who lived in states with different presidential primary timings (as shown in Table 3.1) across the country. The variations in state primary elections are vast:

- some states have more delegates than others,
- some states allocate delegates in a winner-takes-all format and some proportionally,
- some candidates are better placed to win some states over others,
- some states are more expensive to campaign in compared to others, and
- early states can be more valuable to win because they affect a candidate's status in the media as being "viable."

These variations in how the primary elections work across states create very real differences for people, in terms of their need to search for political information. Two people who want to vote on Super Tuesday and live in different states may have differing needs to search for information around election time because there may be great variation in how much campaign activity—advertising and political canvassing—is being done by the candidates in their own state. However, regardless of these campaign effects and the effects of events in the national news, individuals still seek out more political information ahead of presidential primary elections, across states and across the primary calendar.

Understanding Campaigning in Primary Elections

Primary elections are difficult to understand because the rules for primaries vary across states and between the two political parties. For example, consider how Super Tuesday worked for Republicans in 2008, where 21 states had primaries on the same day. If you look at the delegate counts, it would seem that winning in California would be more valuable than winning in any other state because California had 173 delegates in the Republican primary compared to 101 in New York or 72 in Georgia (the third most valuable state on Super Tuesday). However, New York is a winner-take-all state statewide—whoever gets the most votes in the Republican primary wins all of the state's delegates—while California is winner-takes-all at the congressional district level. A candidate might not be able to win all of California but could win a couple of districts and collect a sizable number of delegates. In New York, winning parts of the state only matters if you win the entire state. There are also much higher campaigning costs in California, a state with 14 designated media markets, four of which have more than 2.1 million people. The Los Angeles media market alone is bigger than the population of every US state except Florida, New York, and Texas; running ads in California's major media markets is expensive. Given these costs, a voter in California might actually have to search online more than a person in a more competitive state, like Georgia, where there might be more advertising on television and radio.

So, let's review the CCAP data to determine who was searching for information online during the primary election season. Remember, we predicted that, for Democrats, women and African Americans would search online less and, for Republicans, we predicted that Mormons and veterans would search less. For the Democrats, we were correct; African American and female respondents were much less likely than others to search for information online. The comedian Larry Wilmore's humorous comments on *The Nightly Show* were correct; the cues that an African American voter could get from Obama also being African American were incredibly powerful. Likewise, women were also able to get strong cues from having a woman on the ballot. Having an African American (Obama) and a woman (Hillary Clinton) running greatly limited the need for women or African Americans to learn about other candidate options. Some of you may be wondering the answer to the obvious question here: which cue was more powerful, the race cue or the gender cue. After all, black women are approximately 8 percentage points more likely to vote compared to black men. According to the *Washington Post*'s analysis of exit polls in state's with large black populations,

> Obama has swamped Clinton among black voters in each of the 20 contests
> that had exit polls and large enough samples of African Americans to be

meaningful. Just to put that kind of shutout in perspective, black voters represent the only demographic group that the New York senator has not carried at least once during the Democratic primary campaign. Obama now has such a lock on the loyalties of African Americans—84 percent of the black vote in Alabama, 87 percent in Georgia, 84 percent in Maryland, and on and on—that the black vote is no longer contestable.[30]

For African American women, race trumped gender in making a vote choice.

Turning to Republicans, we see that individuals with a military association or association with the Mormon faith were *more likely* to read about politics online. There are likely several reasons for these two groups to search more. For veterans, there is the fact that being a veteran is not a visible characteristic; knowing whether a person served is something one has to search to determine. In addition, the 2008 election occurred when the conflicts in Iraq and Afghanistan were ongoing. Veterans may be more likely to have followed politics because they wanted to follow events related to these conflicts. For Mormons, the candidacy of Governor Mitt Romney was the first time a Mormon had run for president as a viable candidate since Governor George Romney (MI) ran for president in 1968. It is likely that following the Romney campaign was, for Mormons, much like following the hometown guy who has become famous. They wanted to know how he was doing because his campaign was important for their community. Finally, it may also be that the cues based on either sharing military service or sharing the Mormon faith were not sufficient to keep them from needing to search for political information. Neither religion nor veteran status cues are visible, unlike the gender and race cues Democrats received. Importantly, all things being equal, there were no differences in search activities based on party identification; Democrats and Republicans engaged in similar information-search activities. Where there is a big difference in search activity is between normal people and political junkies. Individuals who have higher political sophistication scores are more likely to report reading about politics online. Political junkies—individuals who are already knowledgeable about politics—needed to keep getting their fix of politics during their sporting season so they used the Internet to stay current with the political ins and outs of the campaign (Carpini 2005). For these junkies, they wanted to know what was going on in the election *regardless of the cues they may have received based on race, gender, or other factors.* It is not surprising that highly sophisticated political use the Internet quite a bit to search for political information. However, even if we take this into account, we still see that search behaviors are strongly affected by the timing of primary elections. Even a political junkie searches more right before their primary election.

GOOGLING DURING THE CALIFORNIA
TOP TWO PRIMARY

Citizens are likely to turn to Google to meet their political information needs. To that end, then, we turn to a very specific case where citizens are likely to have a hard time making a political choice: the California top two primary election. In June 2010, the California voters passed Proposition 14, which shifted the state from a partisan primary system in which one candidate from each party would face each other in the general election to a nonpartisan top two primary format. Within the new primary format, all the candidates for the congressional and state elective offices of all the parties are listed on the primary ballot. All voters then cast votes, regardless of party affiliation. The two candidates who receive the highest number of votes within the primary then move on to face each other in the general election, even if they have the same party label. The new primary system, inevitably, periodically leads to candidates of the same party campaigning against one another within the general election. These co-partisan contests provide a unique opportunity to study how voters might rely on Google to solve a difficult political information problem. Voters can no longer rely on partisan labels. How, then, can they decide for whom to vote in a co-partisan general election? One possibility is that voters can seek out information about the co-partisan candidates online.

Relying on Google Trends data, Sinclair and Wray (2015) look at the rate at which Californians search for the names of California assembly candidates in the 2012 California election cycle. In particular, those voters whose districts present them with same-party general election candidates without the convenience of party labels, are confronted with a more nuanced election in which party identity fails to provide low-cost cues for voters. Records of Internet searches conveniently provide the unique opportunity to quantify the public's search for political knowledge in these low-information environments. They compare online searches for legislative winners who either faced or did not face a co-partisan general election challenger.[31] A difference in search volume when candidates face co-partisan challengers as opposed to candidates from opposing parties suggests that the new top two primary generates a low-information environment in which voters seek out relevant information directly. It also suggests that voters are able to meet the requirements of that election via online political access. Looking at Google Trends data on 109 legislators, 72 members of the State Assembly and 37 members of the State Senate, they find having a co-partisan challenger in the general election is associated with between 13% and 15% increases in Google (scaled) searches in the state of California ahead of the general election. It appears that voters are indeed meeting the demands of their participatory democracy and searching for relevant political information. Looking at a specific example, voters in the 76th state assembly district in California faced a difficult choice for representative in the November 2012 general election, as their ballot included the names of two co-partisan Republicans candidates, Rocky Chavez and Sherry Hodges. Both Republican candidates were relatively similar. During the months leading up to the general election, Google searches for Chavez and Hodges increased by 30 and 50 percent, respectively.

In general, this kind of primary reform—a more open primary—is designed to allow more moderate candidates to be elected. Yet this kind of institution is only possible if voters can identify the more moderate candidates! Finding the right set of political information is a challenging task for voters without a party cue. Here, having online political information meets a key need in allowing these kinds of open primary institutions to function.

GOOGLING DURING PRESIDENTIAL ELECTIONS

Our 2008 study allows us to directly compare the patterns we observe in *Google* searches with individual-level survey data. That we observe similar behavior in both data sources gives us more confidence that the survey respondents are accurately reporting their online behavior and furthermore that the trends we observe in Google searches accord with changes in political interest among the electorate. With that said, we now turn to looking at the aggregate Google data for the 2004, 2008, and 2012 elections to get a sense of search patterns for the entire country. We focus on those searches that included the term "vote." In Figure 3.1 we display, graphically, the search volume for the word "vote" in the United States.

Three very distinct peaks are visible in this figure, corresponding to October 2004, October 2008, and November 2012. That is, national searches for "vote" are greatest during presidential election cycles. The next set of peaks is associated (with the exception of February 2008) with elections as well: November 2006, November 2010, and November 2014. Americans, it appears, are much more likely to search for terms related to voting around elections. This feature corresponds with a rising body of literature that documents the association between Google search and actual political behavior. For example, Street et al. (2015) find that Americans are more likely to search for terms relating to voter registration immediately ahead of voter registration deadlines. In this chapter, we have found that in the 2008 primary elections Americans are responsibly bearing the burdens of democracy, searching out information about elections ahead of politically salient events. We observe similar spikes in searching ahead of national elections as well.

To what extent is increased searching associated with increased participation? In Figure 3.2 we plot the association between a state's presidential voter turnout and its proportion of Google searches associated with the word "vote" in

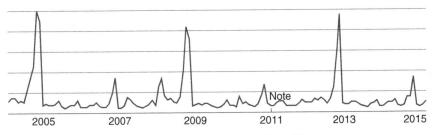

Figure 3.1 Google Search Volume for the Term: Vote, United States
SOURCE: Hall and Sinclair, Google

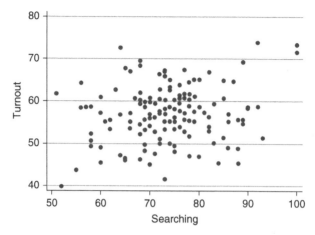

Figure 3.2 Association Between State Search Volume for "Vote" and Voter Turnout in Presidential Elections 2012, 2008, 2004

SOURCE: Hall and Sinclair, Google

the months of October and November, capturing the searches completed during the 2012, 2008, and 2004 presidential elections.[32]

The Google search volume for the word "vote" is positively associated with the presidential turnout rate of the state. What does this say about voters? One important caveat when viewing this data is to remember that this data reflects an aggregate correlation—we have no way to know, for example, if those individuals who are conducting these searches are in fact also voters. Yet, what we can glean from this data is some sense of consistency with our earlier work. We saw in our survey data that voters are indeed using online resources to obtain information about presidential candidates ahead of primary elections. While this fact may seem unsurprising, it is the case that the political science baseline expectation is that voters are largely uninformed about politics and fairly unwilling to bear costs to obtain information about candidates. That we observe so much seeking for specific political information ahead of salient political events challenges that baseline assumption.

Finally, we see search volume for the 2016 presidential primary candidates following the exact trends we described in 2008. Let us focus on the search volume ahead of the 2016 the New Hampshire primary and compare this to the presidential primary vote totals in a figure produced by Simon Rogers, data editor of Google's News Lab team, shown here as Figure 3.3.

Bernie Sanders won the Democratic primary with 60% of the vote in New Hampshire and had 72% of the searches, while Hillary Clinton got 38% of the vote and 28% of the searches. This was also true in the Republican contest. The top-searched Republican candidate was Donald Trump, who won with 35% of the vote. On Google he received 41% of the searches. Next was John Kasich, who got 16% of both the vote and the searches. Ted Cruz took third with 12% of the vote and 15% of the searches. Bush and Rubio were close, but flipped

New Hampshire primary: Search and votes

	% of search, hour before polls close	% of votes
Donald Trump	41.0%	35.0%
John Kasich	16.0%	16.0%
Ted Cruz	15.0%	12.0%
Marco Rubio	10.0%	11.0%
Jeb Bush	7.0%	11.0%
Chris Christie	5.0%	7.0%
Carly Fiorina	4.0%	4.0%
Ben Carson	2.0%	2.0%

Figure 3.3 Search Volume in the 2016 Presidential Primary in New Hampshire
SOURCE: Simon Rogers, Google

positions: Bush took fourth place at the polls (11%) but online 7% while Rubio got 10% of the searches and 10.6% of the vote.

GOOGLE AND DEMOCRATIC VALUES

Now that we have shown how people use Google to search for information online, we can again consider how the Internet and social media are changing how people participate in politics. It is important to remember that, as we have discussed in this chapter, citizens often do not need encyclopedic knowledge in order to be effective citizens. What the Internet can do is provide people with the information that they need to be informed enough to make an effective voting decision. So, when we consider the first question we posed in chapter 1, we can say that new media can decrease the information gap between more-informed and less-informed voters because less-informed voters can find the basic information they need (when it comes to voting). The well-informed do stay better informed but, given that there is a relatively low threshold of information needed to become informed enough to vote, the less-well-informed can easily get the information they need online.

When we consider the broader questions posed in the Preface, we see in this chapter that some cleavages do remain when we consider the use of Google in politics but these cleavages are not across political/ideological lines. The constant availability of information does allow people to choose better representatives, because the data are out there for people to make choices and people are searching for those data. The Google data also suggest that new media is helping the average citizen do their part to be a responsible member of our participatory democracy. Unlike in the past, where access to information would be limited to the three major broadcast news channels—ABC, CBS, and NBC—new media allow people to access print and television news quickly and easily. You don't have to live in New York to get the *New York Times* or in Washington, DC, to get the *Washington Post*. Today, anyone can subscribe to these papers and can access many of the articles for free. Politicians know that people can find information about them, and so have an incentive to maintain a consistent narrative between how they campaign and how they govern.

New media provide people with opportunities to follow politics in great detail on an hourly basis if they want. People can read *Politico* or follow any number of political sites and Twitter feeds and know every small bit of idle chatter going on in DC, in their own state capital, or their own city. A small number of political junkies do this, and these people know who is "up" or "down" at any given time. Most people, however, keep up with the basics of the news but this keeping up also includes knowing about sports, the entertainment industry, and their own personal interests.

However, for specific kinds of events, such as a competitive presidential primary election, individuals need to engage in some amount of information search before voting in order to cast an informed vote. Simple party cues cannot be used in this context to help a voter make a choice. Instead, individuals have to engage in some amount of information search before voting. We found that, in 2008, 65.48% of respondents in the CCAP survey reported that, during at least one of the waves, they had used the Internet to read about politics. Potential voters were not glued to the news during the primary election season; we are not a nation of political news junkies. Instead, people strategically use the Internet to search for information about politics when it is most relevant to them—before their own state's presidential primary election.

The Internet makes accessing political information easier than before because a person can search for information outside of traditional media—evening news and daily newspapers and outside traditional campaign activities—political ads and other contacting. The ability to seek out information online allows more citizens to cast more informed votes. Using Google Trend data, we find that citizens are becoming informed about politics online ahead of state presidential primary elections. Looking at CCAP survey data, we see consistent evidence that individuals self-report using the Internet to read about politics ahead of their state primary as well. Not surprisingly, individuals who already have high levels of political knowledge are more likely to read about politics. However, we do find that, even controlling for political knowledge, individuals are engaging in political Internet use. It is not just those individuals who already have high levels of political knowledge who are searching for political information.

Our research challenges usefulness of the traditional measurement of political knowledge. Estimating an individual's level of political knowledge can seem simple at first glance. Answering more factual questions about politics correctly should correspond with more political knowledge, and fewer correct answers should correspond with less political knowledge. The motivation for the political behavior field is to estimate political knowledge and to understand the extent to which citizens are responsibly bearing the burdens of participatory democracy. We find that individuals, both those with high and those with low levels of political knowledge, are searching for political information online. Of course, the fact that this search process occurs does not tell us whether individuals are more likely to cast "correct" votes, selecting candidates who reflect their ideological positions and any strategic voting considerations they have. However, it does tell us a great deal about the political awareness of these primary voters. If someone knows enough to conduct a Google search about a candidate, do they need to know factual questions about government? Does their factual knowledge about government impact their ability to evaluate what is or is not true online?

Our findings also suggests that there is much to still be learned about how individuals use the Internet for information search. For example, we do not know what types of heuristics and sources individuals use when they read about politics online and what cues are important for shaping an individual's vote choice. We also do not know whether individuals are susceptible to the "supply" of political information provided in their state by campaigns and whether this decreases their "demand" for other types of political information, including information online. Finally, we know little at all about what factors may make an individual less likely to vote. Online information might make a person think voting in their state's primary is irrelevant because one candidate has already "won" the nomination or because cue-givers may tell them there are not differences between the candidates. This type of query is particularly interesting to consider in the context of open primary elections such as the California top two primary, where the critical online exchange of information is not only about facts but also about the likely actions of other voters. Examination of these and other questions is needed for a true picture of the role of the Internet and politics to emerge. What we do systematically observe is that indeed voters are seeking out political information online.

Political campaigns care deeply about how voters obtain this information. In January of 2016, Google produced a new search tool to match searchers with content generated by campaigns.[33] The presidential candidates of both parties can produce content that will appear in a special window on the results page when a user conducts a relevant search. Whether or not this information is truly critical to establishing political behaviors or changing political attitudes is uncertain, and political scientists are still trying to sort through the entertainment value of political searches from the informative value of political searches. For example, after Donald Trump emerged victorious after the 2016 "Super Tuesday" election, there was a dramatic surge in Google searches for "move to Canada."[34] Moving to Canada is probably an idle threat. But journalists and scholars are genuinely interested in the patterns of search volume for election-related terms, and many believe that by capturing searches for presidential candidates, policy issues, and current events that these search patterns will be predictive of true political choices.[35]

We see strong evidence here that Americans will seek out political information via new media and, most importantly, that they will do so ahead of politically salient events. When we think of critical tests to evaluate whether the data we observe on Google Trends parallels actual data, we consistently find a strong correlation between what is happening online and offline. That is, real-world turnout parallels searching for the word "vote." Self-reported searching patterns parallel spikes in searching online in the 2008 presidential primary. Search volume for

2016 presidential candidates parallels the primary election outcomes. While any one example might not be conclusive, the significant body of evidence we have accumulated in this chapter should be persuasive that the behavioral patterns we observe online are real. Moreover, these behavioral patterns are incredibly positive—they indicate that indeed citizens are dutifully acquiring the political information they need. They go online, and they figure out how to cast an informed vote. There are increasingly opportunities for civic-minded technologies to build up and help Americans become informed about voting. We have seen a revolution, for example, in how Americans can use voting advice applications in forming their political preferences (Alvarez, Levin, Mair, et al. 2014; Alvarez, Levin, Trechsel, et al. 2014). These are online surveys, essentially, where voters can respond to a series of questions and have a computer program sift through the candidates to identify who most closely aligns with a voter's personal preferences. The empirical evidence suggests that voters who use them find them helpful. Note that none of these applications teach information about civics; instead, they help voters sift through a world of information quickly and efficiently to vote correctly. We next turn to a different kind of political information acquisition: the notion of a deliberative forum. New media provided not only access to information but also typically access to a user community. We are particularly interested in whether these communities meet the normative goals of deliberative forums.

SUGGESTED READINGS

Reilly, Shauna, Sean Richey, and J. Benjamin Taylor. 2012. "Using Google Search Data for State Politics Research: An Empirical Validity Test Using Roll-Off Data." *State Politics and Policy Quarterly* 12(2): 146– 159.

Lazer, David, Ryan Kennedy, Gary King, and Alessandro Vespignani. 2014. "The Parable of Google Flu: Traps in Big Data Analysis" *Science* 343 (176): 1203–1205.

Carpini, M., and S. Keeter. 1996. *What Americans Know About Politics and Why It Matters*. Yale University Press.

CHAPTER 4

Debating Politics in the YouTube Comments Section

A 28-year-old man (a "scant TV watcher") watches the Bernie Sanders "America" campaign ad via his phone on YouTube. After watching the video on his morning commute, the viewer tears up. He is so touched that he posts a link to the video on his Facebook status and explicitly shares it with his mother, asking her to watch it as well.[1] This anecdote—as described in a *Washington Post* article—is the kind campaigns were hoping would happen with YouTube; online media providing a new channel for political communication. Before the 2016 presidential election, it seemed unlikely that YouTube would become an influential political channel. Indeed, the most-watched YouTube videos are dance videos like "Gangnam Style" (2,551,961,231 views); music videos from Taylor Swift, Mark Rondon, or Adele; or sing-along videos such as "Frozen" from Disney. These videos have garnered over 200 million views each. To contrast with the Bernie Sanders video described above, the Sanders "America" video has received a total of 3,501,190 views.[2] This is still a large number, but it illustrates the point that political videos are not the most captivating videos on YouTube, and that more people are interested in dance videos than political videos. Fundamentally the primary function of YouTube is not political.[3] Yet YouTube is increasingly serving a political purpose. In 2008, Hilary Clinton announced her presidential candidacy by posting a video on her webpage in a revolutionary move.[4] Just eight years later, all the 2016 presidential primary candidates posted campaign announcement videos on YouTube. Campaigns hope the YouTube user community will be entertained by these videos, learn from them, be persuaded or mobilized by them, and perhaps even comment on them and share them with others. YouTube has over 1 billion viewers; some fraction of these viewers want to be engaged in politics.

After each YouTube video there is a space for public comments. Additionally, it is possible to reply to a specific comment. People are not born good citizens. Learning how to responsibly bear the burdens of participatory democracy requires basic civics training. How do you reason about politics? Do you consider your own interests, or the interests of others? What kind of society is fair? What are the ways you can participate? One avenue to engage in politics is by watching YouTube videos. As of April 2016, Donald Trump's presidential announcement had been watched more than 1.8 million times, for example. More 18- to 49-year-olds watch YouTube videos on their phone than tune into any cable network in America, Nielsen data show. YouTube is now ubiquitous as a way to consume political content. Moreover, you can comment on that content directly, within a user community.

YouTube videos provide a specific way to study new media, because they combine two components of the new media revolution that we particularly want to focus on in our analysis. First, they provide users with information, and importantly, this information often comes directly from the candidates themselves. One of the great promises of new media is that it eliminates the "middle man" in political communication—political candidates can speak directly to their constituents. Through recorded videos of speeches, these candidate speeches can be viewed whenever their constituents find it convenient and necessary to make a good electoral choice. One way to evaluate the importance of something like YouTube political videos in the context of the new media revolution is simply to look at who is using them to acquire political information. We come back to this question in chapter 6. To summarize, though, there is a significant proportion of American voters who rely on YouTube as a political information source: about 13.5%.

The second component, however, is the focus of this chapter. We are particularly interested in the relationships that can be established within the YouTube user community. The readily accessible cornucopia of information via new media is the predominant focus of most studies. To what extent are people's political behaviors and attitudes influenced by the user communities that are established as part of these new media political information resources? Many videos on YouTube allow comments by viewers. Is there any evidence that engaging with this community changes people's political behaviors and attitudes? Our goal in this analysis is simply to describe what the typical behavior in the YouTube comment community looks like and, in particular, to hold this up against the normative ideals of a democratic, deliberative forum.

Democratic theorists have long considered the necessary and sufficient conditions by which a democratic government can be sustained. The primary argument of these theorists is that democracy is sustained not merely by voting but also by conversation: authentic deliberation and consensus decision-making generate support for the rule of law, even for dissidents. One of the hopes of those who applauded the arrival of the new media revolution was that these online communities could provide a new space for political deliberation. Evidence that users are abiding by the tenets of deliberative democracy would suggest that new media has indeed improved the quality of governance through the establishment of these new media communities.

YouTube provides a particularly unique opportunity to evaluate the extent to which people engage in political deliberation. Talking about politics in a meaningful way where there are actual consequences (such as a collective decision) that the group must bear is frequently referred to as deliberative democracy. One avenue for people to both learn about politics and engage as responsible citizens is through political deliberation. In some very real sense YouTube is ideally suited to test theories of political deliberation. All the text is written and easily collectable. Users are relatively immune to the pressures of social position or talk time. Indeed, users can reply to comments posted hours earlier or in that same minute.

Yet, YouTube is known for terrible comments. Indeed, the webpage BuzzFeed reports that YouTube has, in fact, the worst quality comments of all online comment feeds.[5] They write, "Content ranges from typed grunts to racist sentence fragments to nonsensical homophobic outbursts. Nothing is off-limits. The only way these comments could be worse is if Google's spam filters stopped working completely." YouTube, though, illustrates the ways in which new media is transforming American political life. From FoxNation to Politico to HuffPo to Facebook to CNN to the *New York Times*, there are communities of individuals who are posting political comments about political content to each other online. It is imperative we understand something about this exchange, not only because it informs our understanding of the impact of new media on political deliberation but also because it helps us understand political deliberation itself.

ONLINE POLITICAL DELIBERATION

Deliberative theorists have long considered basic questions to understand the parameters under which meaningful and quality political deliberation can occur. There are four features critical to quality deliberation: public-spiritedness, equal respect, accommodation, and equal participation (Thompson 2008). Public-spirited reasoning is "directed toward the collective good of the group that will be bound by the decision." Many online platforms that allow comments may fail at ensuring those comments meet the threshold of public-spirited reasoning, but this does not necessarily imply that the exchange is uncivil. The sole requirement for enabling democracy is that the comment not be focused on self-interest. Equal respect requires that comments be presented "in terms that are accessible to the relevant audience and respond to reasonable arguments presented by opponents." Accommodation requires the comments "keep open the possibility of cooperation on other issues." In an anonymous world of online comments this seems possible. Finally, equal participation requires that "no one person or group will dominate the reason-giving process, even if the deliberators are not strictly equal in power and prestige" (Thompson 2008: 504–505). This seems eminently possible via online comments. Thus an online public forum such as those that follow online political content seems quite suited to meet the requirements to allow meaningful political deliberation. They have an added benefit as well. While some political scientists have tried to empirically evaluate the features and effects of political deliberation, they typically do so in an artificial environment away from meaningful collective decisions and in a controlled space, such as in a student laboratory. Looking at deliberation in an actual online forum adds external validity to our study, as we focus on the kinds of deliberative arguments that are offered sincerely (and from fully volunteer participants) ahead of an actual election. True deliberation requires its users to reach a collective decision. In this case, then, online comments provide a terrific avenue to test theories of deliberation if we focus on the presidential primary election and comments surrounding that particular online content. Political deliberation surrounding future elections is a discussion where the users do indeed need to reach a collective decision.

The initial promise of online political deliberation was that it would provide a common public sphere where individuals, stripped down to anonymous strangers in structurally equivalent social positions, could engage in inclusive, meaningful conversation. These spaces would provide the opportunity for true political deliberation, where the potential effects of high-quality online public discourse could meaningfully change attitudes and behaviors as a consequence of seriously considered democratic principles. Yet, as anyone who has ever read a set of online comments knows, this seems laughable. The comments sections from a news article, or a YouTube video, are frequently vicious, mean, and anti-intellectual.

Although the Internet has increased opportunities for participants to voice their opinions and to engage in conversation with others, there is a question as to whether there is actual online deliberation. The barriers to deliberation and democratic learning online are X-fold. First, incivility online can affect the willingness of people to engage in democratic debate. Second, it can affect how people perceive an issue.

INCIVILITY AND PERCEPTION

One major problem with coarse discourse online, especially in online comments, is that it can actually affect both people's willingness to engage in debate and the ways in which people perceive the issue being debated. Before delving into how people engage ideas online or offline, it is important to consider what we mean by incivility. In her 2004 work, Papacharissi notes, "conversations on the meaning of citizenship, democracy, and public discourse highlight civility as a virtue, [but] the actual meaning of civility tends to be rather elusive." She notes that civility literature tends to focus on behaviors, reducing civility to being polite in a debate, instead of focusing on the merits of what is being debated and the quality of the debate. If the goal of a conversation or debate is to promote democratic goals and values, then the issues have to be debated thoroughly, often pressing on difficult questions. When the parties who are debating and discussing are focused on politeness, it will likely result in contentious issues being avoided and a very narrow discussion occurring. Quite simply, in a world where civil equals polite, there cannot be a robust civil discussion that builds democratic capital. There are often times where heated exchanges of ideas need to occur because of the importance of the issue.

Long before there was an Internet, there were heated discussions that built democratic capital. The civil rights protests of the 1960s—although nonviolent—were considered by many to be uncivil; after all, they were disruptive toward businesses, caused many people to feel uncomfortable, and addressed difficult issues about race in society. Yet few would argue that there was not a benefit that came from such confrontational debates. For Papacharissi (2004), the issue is not the politeness of the conversation but whether the discussion takes place and whether this discussion improves our understanding of democracy and its goals.

This idea of incivility as a force that impedes informed deliberation is one that has been studied since before the Internet existed. Mutz and Reeves (2005) have found that incivility in American politics has been on the rise for the past half century. Prior (2007) has found that that the way the media covers issues focusing on conflict and in many cases fanning the flames of that conflict is one reason why political polarization has increased. In modern politics, incivility has become expected and encouraged, in candidate debates in elections, in congressional debates, in print media, and in television (e.g., Uslaner 1993; Funk 2001; Jamison 1997; Sigelman and Bullock 1991; Nisbet and Scheufele 2007). Individual actors in politics may benefit from such incivility, with television shows earning higher ratings when they air contentious debates, and individual politicians scoring points on their opponents through uncivil debate. However, when the public is presented with this sort of uncivil debate—debates that are both superficial and impolite—it harms political institutions such as the Congress, politicians as a group, and the public's trust in its institutions and leaders (Cappella and Jamieson 1997; Mutz and Reeves 2005).

Given the incivility that has existed in American politics for some time, it is not surprising that online debate also shows signs of incivility. Most research has been rather discouraging with respect to the failures of online political forums. Few report online political forums lead to better political discussion. In fact, there is some research to suggest that even the exposure to political disagreement could serve not to galvanize participation but instead to discourage it (Mutz 2002). Anderson et al. (2014) use the term the "nasty effect" to describe the impact of uncivil or offensive commentary on readers who have just read an article online. In a study of the impact of online comments on readers of a blog post, Anderson and colleagues had people read a story about nanotechnology, a topic deliberately chosen because it is complicated, not a topic on which most people are well-read, and rather technical. The tone of the article was neutral, presenting information about both sides of the issue in a scientific manner. After reading the article, people gave their views of nanotechnology and its risks. One group of people only read the article but a second group was exposed to comments that were uncivil, with some being just name calling and others questioning the values of the author of the post and also suggesting that nanotechnology was risky. Not surprisingly, those who were exposed to the hostile commentary were more likely to have a perception that nanotechnology was risky, and this was especially true for individuals with high levels of religiosity.

Debate is also more contentious when people can comment anonymously. As Suler (2004, 321) notes, "People say and do things in cyberspace that they wouldn't ordinarily say and do in the face-to-face world." He notes the anonymity of the Internet allows people to create an online persona that is separate from their own. Being able to dissociate ourselves with what we say online and to create an online persona allows people to engage in what Suler calls "dissociative imagination"—their online persona is almost an alter ego who says things that they would never say if they were subject to the social cues that come from a face-to-face discussion and felt that their behavior was being observed and judged. On Twitter, people are more likely to reply to people who share the same view (Yardi and Boyd 2010). Online media may also increase polarization by enabling consumers to self-select into homogeneous discussion environments (Lelkes et al. 2015). The discussion bubble extends beyond conversations with other peers—citizens may also avoid contacting legislators who do not share their partisan views (Broockman and Ryan 2015). These are some of the perilous consequences from allowing consumer sovereignty (Sunstein 2001) in online public spheres: by letting an individual's preferences guide her choices for public commons, the public commons themselves serve to provide a biased information diet that encourages her political ideology to drift away from a moderate position. These findings should not be surprising to people who have studied the psychology related to processing information. Most people have a set of beliefs and values that define who they are as a person and in which they are invested. Numerous studies have found that, when people are confronted with information that conflicts with their beliefs and values, they are likely to discount the veracity of the new information. In the language of blackjack, many people will double down on their original belief, believing even more that they are correct in the face of new information. People who are more ideological are likely to double down, as are people who are more religious.[6]

How, then, can online political discussion contribute to democratic decision-making? The Internet has brought a myriad of opportunities for participants to voice their opinions and to engage in conversation with others. From Reddit to the *New York Times*, online commons allow users to post messages. To what extent do we observe online deliberation in these online commons? Are individuals simply espousing their opinion in a public space, as if posting a flyer? Or instead do we see evidence that people are engaging the opinions of others? That is, where do we see comments posted in response?

In this chapter we focus on one specific case to better understand online political deliberation. We focus on YouTube comments. First, we look at the patterns of responses and likes on the 2016 presidential campaign announcements on YouTube. We hope to evaluate whether there is evidence that YouTube comment sections can serve as a venue to provide meaningful political deliberation. There is some reason to believe that this is the case. Kelly et al. 2005, analyzing political newsgroups, finds that "the strongest conversational links are across political divides" (23) and that, moreover, comment authors are frequently found to be in conversation with their ideological opponents (Kelly et al. 2005). While YouTube comments surely miss the theoretical aims of a shared discussion space in terms of quality and civility, there is an argument to be made that the incivility and dissonance are in fact evidence of true political conversation: the contestation is one argumentative strategy toward persuasion (Broncheck 1997; Papacharissi 2004). Perhaps people go online to argue with others, but this engagement is informative. Perhaps instead people go online simply to shout their opinion but do little listening. We hope to evaluate the quality of these forums. Second, we look at the population of YouTube commenters who have written posts on YouTube videos for Hillary Clinton or Donald Trump speeches. We are particularly interested in looking at an ensemble of videos, as we want to know something about the repeat posters. How many times do they post on videos? Do they post across videos? Do they post on both Clinton and Trump videos? To what extent are they engaging anonymously or are they instead identifying other users in their comments? These are a handful of questions we address in this chapter.

YOUTUBE

Our target population for evaluating whether or not there is evidence of online political deliberation is the YouTube user community: those individuals who watch and comment on one of the 2016 presidential campaign announcements. This provides us with a target group that is commenting on political content across a spectrum of ideological positions. We are particularly interested in three features. First, we simply document the rate of replies to what YouTube calls top-level comments—an initial post that is not necessarily a reply to a previous post. This is a measurement for direct participation in the conversation. Second, we look at the rate of "liked" comments in contrast to the rate of replies: to what extent are users indicating their approval without providing commentary—a very unique feature of online forums. This is a measurement of how people are in fact reading the conversation but not necessarily joining in. In particular this is distinct from the number of "views" that any particular YouTube video would have. Finally, we look at the profiles of the user community itself. How frequently are the same individuals writing? To what extent do they post across political lines?

We collected all top-level YouTube comments for the presidential campaign announcement video for the following 2016 presidential primary candidates on February 10, 2016: Bush, Carson, Clinton, Cruz, Rubio, Sanders, and Trump. A top-level comment is one that initiates a conversation: other users can then reply to that comment. This gave us a total of 4,693 comments. One thing to note is that not all official campaign videos enable comments: The Clinton campaign, for example, enables comments while the Trump campaign did not. This means that we use the video released by the Clinton campaign on the Hillary Clinton YouTube channel in our analysis but we do not do this for the Trump campaign. Instead, we identified a video covering his presidential campaign announcement that also enables comments. That is, for each candidate, if their campaign had not identified an official YouTube video we chose the C-SPAN announcement video that covered their announcement that they were entering the 2016 presidential primary. Our goal here is to choose videos that are similar both in terms of content and in terms of prominence, with the hope that an interested YouTube community member would want to watch all of these videos and could expect a similar comment-community for each video in terms of political interest and engagement.

How can you collect YouTube comment data? YouTube produces an application programming interface (API) that significantly simplifies the process to collect comments from specific YouTube videos. This API allows you to get comments posted on YouTube videos, information on how many times a video has been viewed, and a number of other key pieces of information. The API is typically used in partnership with a software program such as R (free!).

Perhaps people go online to argue with others. Barbera et al. (2015) find significant evidence of cross-ideological engagement on Twitter and suggest previous work may have overestimated the degree of ideological segregation in social-media usage.

The content of the comments is fairly obnoxious: the level of vitriol in each You-Tube post is fairly remarkable. For example, on the Clinton presidential statement one user writes, "HILLARY, WE'VE TOLD YOU NO ALREADY. BE A GOOD GIRL AND GO TO THE TIME-OUT CORNER," and another writes, "seriously, why not vote for the man who's gonna keep the moslems and mexicans out of the US?" Can this be a forum where political conversation takes place? We begin by presenting a very simple summary of our data. We identify the portion of repeat posters, and for each post, identify the number of "replies" and the number of "likes."

First, we focus on the individuals who post repeatedly. We plot the histogram of repeat users in Figure 4.1. We have a preponderance of individuals who post only once. The average rate of top-level comments per user is just over one: the average number of top level comments per user is 1.4 for Bush, 1.3 for Carson, 1.5 for Clinton, 1.2 for Cruz, 1.6 for Rubio, 1.3 for Sanders, and 1.4 for Trump. There is a great deal of variation across candidates, however. Clinton has the greatest number of repeat posters (31), with Bush coming in second (with 15). Cruz and Sanders, on the other hand, have only a handful of individuals who post more than once. We can also see this pattern supported in the standard deviation in Table 4.1. Across videos we have the greatest total number of comments for Clinton (2,674) and this corresponds with the greatest total views (728,815) and total times the video has been shared (3,623). Interestingly we see slightly more comments for Bush but than for any candidate other than Clinton, but Carson has the next highest number of total views and total shares.

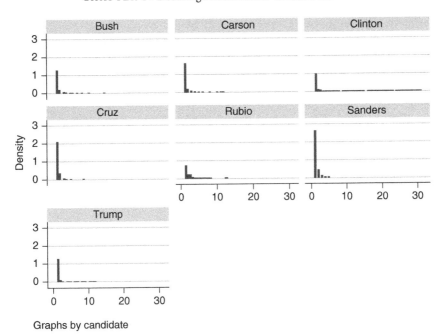

Graphs by candidate

Figure 4.1 Frequency of Specific User Comments for 2016 Presidential Announcement YouTube Videos
SOURCE: Hall and Sinclair, YouTube

Table 4.1 Top Level Comment Rate
Each individual user makes slightly more than one comment on average, but the variation in comment rate by candidate is quite large.

CANDIDATE	OBSER- VATIONS	MEAN	STANDARD DEVIATION	MIN	MAX	TOTAL VIEWS	TOTAL SHARES
Bush	489	1.41	1.19	1	15	89,852	409
Carson	468	1.33	1.14	1	12	228,421	2312
Clinton	2674	1.49	2.23	1	31	728,815	3623
Cruz	428	1.22	.62	1	9	93,622	857
Rubio	178	1.61	1.40	1	13	136,202	425
Sanders	184	1.26	.61	1	5	58,329	466
Trump	272	1.40	1.46	1	12	70,699	448

Source: Hall and Sinclair, YouTube

We next evaluate the rate of replies and likes by candidate in Figure 4.2 through Table 4.3. Here we are focusing on the number of replies we observe for the top-level comments and the number of instances a comment has been liked. Videos with greater numbers of comments have, arguably, the best chance for replies and likes. In terms of an average reply rate, this is not true for Clinton. Cruz, Carson, and

Sanders—all of whom have fewer total comments, have a higher average number of responses to those top-level comments. Clinton has generated more variation in her comment pattern; looking at Figure 4.2, it is clear that she has more comments that have more replies, and in fact her maximum number of comments is 342, much higher than any of the other candidates. Clinton continues to have high rates of likes and a higher standard deviation with respect to likes of top comments, as seen in Table 4.3, but here is also able to generate the second-largest like rate of all

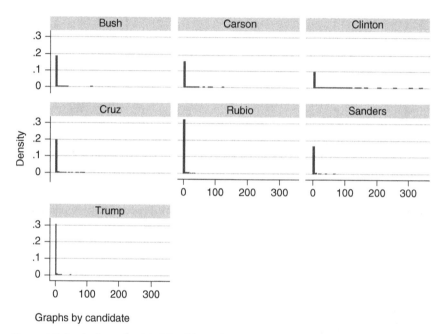

Graphs by candidate

Figure 4.2 Reply Count for 2016 Presidential Announcement YouTube Videos
SOURCE: Hall and Sinclair, YouTube

Table 4.2 Top Level Comment Reply Rate
Each top-level comment generates a range of responses, with Cruz having the highest average number of replies.

CANDIDATE	OBSERVATIONS	MEAN	STANDARD DEVIATION	MIN	MAX
Bush	489	1.08	6.41	0	113
Carson	468	2.18	9.70	0	125
Clinton	2674	1.63	13.81	0	342
Cruz	428	2.82	11.11	0	91
Rubio	178	1.40	4.68	0	36
Sanders	184	2.25	7.07	0	70
Trump	272	.86	3.87	0	49

Source: Hall and Sinclair, YouTube

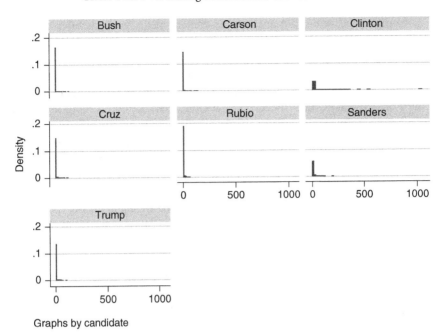

Graphs by candidate

Figure 4.3 Like Count for 2016 Presidential Announcement YouTube Videos
SOURCE: Hall and Sinclair, YouTube

Table 4.3 Top Level Comment Like Rate
Each top-level comment generates a range of responses, with Sanders having the highest average number of likes.

CANDIDATE	OBSERVATIONS	MEAN	STANDARD DEVIATION	MIN	MAX
Bush	489	2.67	12.37	0	126
Carson	468	2.72	12.94	0	138
Clinton	2674	3.94	32.17	0	1047
Cruz	428	3.37	11.85	0	122
Rubio	178	2.58	8.05	0	62
Sanders	184	8.52	23.87	0	198
Trump	272	2.92	11.57	0	109

Source: Hall and Sinclair, YouTube

candidates. Sanders, with an average of 8.52 likes on top comments posted to his video, has the greatest number. In general the high like rate for Sanders is similar to what others are finding on Facebook and other social media. An analysis by US Uncut found that Sanders received 42% of Facebook mentions compared to 13% for Clinton. Yet Sanders garnered less than a third of the press attention that Clinton attracted on traditional media. For particular subgroups of voters, social media allows them to engage in politics without relying on traditional media structures.[7]

In this data, we did not analyze the content of the posts themselves. This means that while we can evaluate the rate of replies within a conversation, we cannot say anything about the quality of that conversation. We cannot distinguish, for example, a conversation that goes along the lines of, "This candidate is a jerk" and a reply that says, "You are a jerk!" from "This candidate's main policy objective is X and I believe our nation needs Y" and a reply that says, "Given our current limitations on the debt ceiling I am concerned about X." Yet, a quick glance through the comments themselves suggests that the quality of the dialogue seems unlikely to instill confidence that this is a forum for political deliberation. What kind of community is an online YouTube comment forum?

When we look at the rate of replies to comments, the rate of likes for comments, and the extent to which the community is re-engaging via new posts, we get some sense of how the typical user engages as part of the YouTube comment community. That is, we are able to learn a great deal simply via descriptive statistics. We do not observe a particularly dense community: the greatest rate of posting new top-level comments is 31 posts on the Clinton page. This surely isn't the primary forum where people are engaging in political conversation. In the 2004 American National Election Studies (ANES), over 80% of respondents reported having a political discussion with a family member, friend or neighbor. Surely those conversations are still forming the bulk of our political deliberation. Yet, that is not to say that online political forums provide no benefit. Whether users are online to argue or to insult or to engage, we do see a fairly significant number of replies to our top-level comments. Thinking about Table 4.2 more generally, it is quite remarkable that the average top-level comment receives more than one reply. Within one standard deviation, Clinton top-level comments could receive up to 16 replies. These are more than passing insults; 16 comments is starting to sound like political engagement. Moreover, these online forums provide a safe space for people to engage more gently: to consume the impolite comments and to like them without having to commit language or explicit public sentiment to support them. Users engage in this: each comment receives at least two (on average) likes and the top comment received over 1,000 likes.

Likes, more than replies to top level comments, have been decried as a kind of "slacktivism," where users could believe they had engaged in politics in a meaningful way with a mere click of a mouse but in fact have done very little in terms of actual engagement. "Slacktivists," it has been decried, purport to want political change but accomplish nothing with "likes" (and then, some claim, avoid actual substantive actions with real costs). There is some research to suggest that in fact those who engage with politics via "likes" and online "slacktivism" indeed do not participate offline in traditional politics (Vitak et al. 2011). Yet a recent survey from Georgetown University noted that slacktivists have an important and nontraditional role in politics: when compared to those who are not online "slacktivists," the "slacktivists" are twice as likely to volunteer their time, are four times more likely to contact their political representatives, and are five times more likely to recruit others to sign a petition (Dixon 2011). Here we are encouraged by the rate of replies but also by the rate of likes: it is one of the opportunities provided by online political content—an alternative form of engagement via new media.

DISCUSSION BUBBLES

Discussion bubbles are one of the main concerns people have with online political deliberation. What if online political conversations happen exclusively between like-minded individuals? How can meaningful political conversations take place? Furthermore, how do these platforms limit our shared political experiences? To address this concern we look at individuals who have posted more than one comment and evaluate the extent to which they have posted a comment on multiple candidate pages. Within our population of commenters, this is a relatively small fraction of total users: just 12% of all top-level commenters have posted at least two top-level comments (456 individuals total). Within that population, we are particularly interested in what portion of individuals have (1) split their comments across candidates, (2) split their comments across same-party candidates, and (3) split their comments across party lines. We find that 63% of the users make all of their top-level comments about a single candidate (288) and that 78% of the users make all of their top-level comments about candidates within the same party (357). This seems like a lot, and it seems that the preponderance of comments are in fact occuring within the same party and moreover within the same candidate. What is remarkable, though, is that remaining 22% of users. They are posting across party lines. They are posting for both Republicans and Democrats on their presidential primary announcement videos.

What are these bipartisan YouTube commenters saying? Remarkably their content allies very closely with those ideals espoused by deliberative theorists. Some of the comments are actual arguments that do not engage self-based reasoning. "Beach Bum" writes on the Clinton, Sanders, and Bush pages that "Bernie Sanders will make America better!" Says "AlexanderTheNotSoGreat" on the Cruz video, "Correct me if I am wrong; this guy was born in Canada, right? So in order to run for US president, you have to be a NATURAL born citizen of the USA, right?" and on the Clinton video, "She is not getting my vote. :)." Similarly, "Alfarojv" says on the Clinton video, "Obama Part 2. Are you ready?" and on the Cruz video, "You brought God into it. You've won my vote sir, America needs REAL change, REAL logic, not fairy tales like believing we and everything evolved from a rock over billions of years. Nothing does not create EVERYTHING ludicrous and absurd. God is in control. Ted for president!" Some of the comments are simply positive. Says "Albert Y" on the Bush video, "Go Jeb, Go!!" and on the Sanders video, "HOPE, I have Hope again!"

To compare the bipartisan commenting community to another set of communities, we turn to data collected by two economists, Jesse Shapiro and Matthew Gentzkow (2011). They calculated the extent to which conservatives were exposed to liberal ideology using actual Internet use data and contrasted this with offline media exposure and face-to-face interactions. Note that this is simply the average exposure to liberal ideology for a conservative person, which is distinct from having a conservative actually deliberating with a liberal person. We observed approximately 20% of the repeat commenters engaging in bipartisan deliberation. This is lower than the rate of exposure that an average individual would have to bipartisan contacts among their political discussants (40%), their broadcast news (60%), or even considering their political Internet use (50%). Thus while the rate of bipartisan posting is higher than we expected, it still pales in comparison to the kinds of exposures an average individual would have in a typical media diet.

CLINTON VERSUS TRUMP SPEECHES: THE YOUTUBE COMMENTERS COMMUNITY

In the previous section we analyzed the comments on the 2016 presidential primary candidate campaign announcement videos. While these videos share a common theme, they do not appear on a single YouTube channel.

A channel on YouTube is the home page for an account. It will show the public videos uploaded into that account, and it is a reasonable way to curate favorite videos.

In order to study the YouTube comment community more broadly, we also selected one specific YouTube channel and focused on the comments from all videos in that channel. We cannot select the candidate channels. The Trump channel has completely disabled comments, and the Clinton channel has almost completely followed suit. Only six videos on Clinton's channel have comments enabled—and moreover, all six videos were posted in the month following the official announcement of her presidential campaign (circa April 12, 2015); only one of which has more than 1,000 comments. In order to provide a good illustration of an active comment community, we selected the channel titled "Donald Trump vs Hillary Clinton Speeches and Events." Though not an official candidate channel, this is a channel that focuses on the 2016 presidential contest and also allows comments. This channel has recordings of full speeches given by the two candidates and their respective running mates. Combined, the channel contains about 230 videos. The Clinton videos date as far back as June 2016, and the Trump videos date back even further, to January 2016. The videos have wildly disparate numbers of comments, from 1 to 3,986, for a total of over 65,000 comments (with an average of 283 per video). What we hope to do is focus on the comments embedded within a channel, to see if perhaps the curation of the channel could generate a more tight-knit YouTube community.

To that end, we turn to descriptive statistics about users. In this dataset we observe 65,466 total comments from 20,586 total users. Of these, about 23% (15,227) are comments that are directed to other users—that is, that are not only replies but are replies where the other user's YouTube name is identified in the comment. Users make an average of 3 comments, ranging from 1 up to 868. Interestingly, the majority of users are writing on more than one video's comments: over 35,000 of the comments are from users who write on more than one video and who post on an average of 5 different video comments. There is a significant amount of more passive participation as well: the 230 videos have, on average, 93 likes and 67 dislikes.

Like our analysis of comments on presidential campaign announcement videos, we observe a higher proportion of engagement in the YouTube videos than we initially expected. When reading through these comments, we recognize that this is a forum that surely does not meet, as characterized by Mutz (2008), the requirements invoked as necessary to have deliberative success, but they may meet the desirable outcomes linked to deliberative processes. That is, YouTube comments fail in terms of "civility" and "face-to-face" and "equality of reason-giving/participation." However, they could arguably increase "awareness of oppositional arguments," "knowledge/information gain/sophistication," and "political self-efficacy." These two YouTube comment communities are small illustrations of the broader world of online communities that have arrived with new media. Despite the vitriol in comment sections, they are not entirely disastrous. There is at least a small amount of evidence of deliberation.

REAL COMMUNICATION ON YOUTUBE

Barack Obama once said YouTube provided "21st century fireside chats where I'm speaking directly to the American people via video streams."[8] Increasingly it is the case that candidates are indeed speaking directly to citizens via YouTube. What do the citizens say about that? Can we use the YouTube comments as a way to evaluate the kinds of online platforms that are available for political deliberation?

Our primary findings are largely encouraging about the capacity of new media to build meaningful political communities. We observe an enormous number of replies and likes on YouTube, despite having a fairly diffuse community of users who seldom post top-level comments. While "likes" could be considered "slacktivism," the term does not necessarily have a pejorative association. YouTube videos provide one way to share political information, and indeed we observe a phenomenal number of viewings of these videos, but this is not so dissimilar to our other findings in our chapters on googling for political information. In general, it is encouraging that the candidates have a mechanism to communicate directly to voters and that the voters are collecting and consuming that information. This increased transparency in the democratic process is a healthy improvement that is a clear win for new media. What is particularly revolutionary about these videos, though, is the sharing of comments from the user community. If the provision of YouTube videos by presidential candidates was only consumed, but not shared or commented on, this would be no different than any other online news source (with the exception that it comes directly from candidates). Even if only to throw insults at each other, the YouTube comments provide an avenue for political engagement between citizens. The quality of the exchange may be particularly low, but the exchange exists. Furthermore, the anonymity of the site and the ability to simply "like" a comment gives a vote to individuals who are otherwise disinclined to participate in traditional politics. Not only is there real communication on YouTube but also the multiple avenues of participation increase the inclusivity of this community.

At the same time, social media sites also continue to face problems with uncivil and hateful commenting. For example, the Republican National Committee had to turn off the chat function on its YouTube livestream party convention because there were so many anti-Semitic comments being made during a speech by the former governor of Hawaii, Linda Lingle. As she spoke about the Republican Party's Jewish outreach efforts and support for Israel, people posted pro–Adolf Hitler comments and Jewish slurs.[9] These types of events, as well as general attacks on women and others online, do suggest the limits of unmoderated online forums. Although most people may want to use such sites for civil debate or informational commenting, these sites face the threat of being overtaken by a small group that uses the sites to promote hate or to undermine discourse generally. Even over the course of the Clinton campaign there was a shift in YouTube comments on the official campaign channel: at some point the comments became so repugnant that it made sense to turn off comments altogether. While there is clearly interest in real political engagement, there is also interest in generating and igniting hate.

Another real risk is the presence of a discussion bubble. While we do observe approximately 20% of the repeat commenters making comments across party lines, this kind of political exposure is much lower than prior measurements of exposure for an average citizen from their standard political information diet of mainstream media, peers, or even the Internet as a whole. Despite the suitability of the platform for potential political deliberation, it is clearly not the case that all voices are heard in equal volume. Yet, it is the case that that minimum standards for political deliberation (at least those set by normative theorists) appear to be met, albeit perhaps not met sufficiently to produce deliberative success.

Robert Putnam (2000) argued that we are increasingly "bowling alone," failing to participate in civic and political activities and abandoning our neighborhood social networks. What if instead we are "bowling online"? What if instead we are interacting with a community of individuals across neighborhoods, across states, and across nations? Can this new kind of online community facilitate quality democratic governance? There are a myriad of online communities, designed for dating, for product reviews, for sharing photos, for sharing important life moments—the list goes on and on. Some of these online communities are structured around politics. They don't seem to have figured out an appropriate policing strategy, so sometimes the online communities are taken over by speech that is hateful and destructive. Yet, online deliberative engagement is present, even in the least-regulated, most vile of forums like YouTube. This, more than anything, is encouraging about the rise of new media. The next revolution needs to be an institutional one, to recover social norms into the space of online speech. It is important to remember that the new media revolution is still nascent. In 2016, we assumed that all the presidential campaigns would produce online videos so that users would hear the candidate announce their candidacy at any time, for their convenience. Yet just 8 years earlier, in 2008, when Senator Clinton announced her campaign in a video on her website on a Saturday morning, with the goal of communicating directly to voters, the *New York Times* covered her strategy, remarking on the unusual political tactic.[10] New media has dramatically changed how we consume political content and what is available to consume. That transformation, combined with the presence of some kind of positive and encouraging findings in YouTube communities, suggests that online communities can and do engage in some kind of political deliberation.

This chapter shows that YouTube provides important information to the public that is used to understand politics. When people can see politicians speak in context, which YouTube facilitates, it helps them make better electoral decisions. We also see that people can deliberate in meaningful ways using YouTube, even though some people do use the platform for posting more inflammatory comments as well. We also see politicians using YouTube to communicate directly to the public, getting their messages out and not needing the news media to get this message out for them.

Ostensibly Twitter would appear to provide a similar kind of community, where users could also reply readily to each other. Yet Twitter seems not to generate the same kind of debate but is more typically used as a way to directly communicate with elites. Here, too, however we see evidence of new media's beneficial influence on democracy. Members of Congress, it appears, are directly communicating their ideology in their Twitter communication. We turn to an evaluation of Twitter in our next chapter on direct communication from political elites in social media.

SUGGESTED READINGS

Cohen, J. L. 2003. "Party over Policy: The Dominating Impact of Group Influence on Political Beliefs." *Journal of Personality and Social Psychology* 85: 808–822.

Fishkin, J. S. 1995. *The Voice of the People: Public Opinion and Democracy*. Yale University Press.

Putnam, R. 2000. *Bowling Alone: The Collapse and Revival of American Community*. Simon and Schuster.

CHAPTER 5

Receiving Tweets from Politicians

In the 2016 presidential election, the unchallenged Twitter champion was Donald Trump. Trump understood that the mainstream media dominates items that trend on Twitter so, by being on there and being bombastic, he could remain first and foremost in the mind of reporters who are tied to it 24/7. He could also speak directly to his supporters and sidestep mainstream media. According to *Politico* on December 6, 2016, the Twitter user @joshrogin tweets, "Dick Cheney praises Trump's going around the press to communicate by tweet: 'We don't need you guys anymore.' #RNDF."

As the *New York Times* has noted,

> Mr. Trump has mastered Twitter in a way no candidate for president ever has, unleashing and redefining its power as a tool of political promotion, distraction, score-settling and attack—and turning a 140-character task that other candidates farm out to young staff members into a centerpiece of his campaign. [Trump] forgoes costly, conventional methods of political communication and relies instead on the free, urgent and visceral platforms of social media. "He's used social media to replace the traditional apparatus of a political campaign," said Zac Moffatt [co-founder of] Targeted Victory, a consulting firm focused on online campaign tactics. "Trump is living on this medium."
>
> [In] two months, on Twitter alone, [Trump] has been mentioned in 6.3 million conversations, eight times as many as [his] Republican rivals—not to mention more than three times as many as Hillary Rodham Clinton and nearly four times as many as Bernie Sanders. He is retweeted more than twice as often as Mrs. Clinton and about 13 times more frequently than Jeb Bush. His Twitter following (4.36 million) dwarfs that of the rest of the Republican field, and in the coming weeks, he is expected to surpass Mrs. Clinton (4.39 million).

It is important to keep in mind that typically primary elections mobilize people who are very political. These are people who follow politics and are very energized generally. Trump's rise to Twitter stardom began during the presidential primary, where his tweets seemed to particularly resonate with his supporters. Indeed, not only did Trump's tweeting give him an ability to speak directly to his followers but also they enabled him to have an increased mainstream media presence.

Trump's social media presence is much like American politics today—bombastic, polarizing, and forceful. He is known for being extremely aggressive online and for having aggressive followers and supporters who amplify this message. So when someone critiques Trump online, Trump may respond, but so will hundreds of his followers. Some of the attacks by his followers can be quite visceral. Rich Lowry, editor of *National Review* (a conservative publication), noted that "I've never encountered an American politician at this level that people are literally afraid of." After *National Review* published a critique of Trump, Lowery said he was the recipient of a flood of hostile Twitter attacks from Mr. Trump's followers after the issue was published, including "some really vile, neo-Nazi-issue white nationalist, heinous personal abuse, kind of racially tinged stuff."

Corey Lewandowski, a Trump campaign manager during the early part of 2016, said his candidate's practice of battering opponents on social media showed that Mr. Trump was "the ultimate counterpuncher," a tough candidate unwilling to take even the slightest criticism lightly. "When someone attacks him, should he just not respond?" Mr. Lewandowski said. "That's not fair."

By starting Twitter wars that his followers then get involved in and continue, Trump successfully mobilized his core supporters and allowed them to feel that they are a part of the campaign on an ongoing basis. As one political operative noted, Trump's engagement "is a continuous Trump rally on Twitter at all hours. He fills the Twitter stadium every day." The ferocity of these attacks by Trump, and the follow-on waves that come from his supporters, also deter some people from criticizing Trump online. By dominating social media, he can get his message out and control the debate in a way that thrills and excites his followers. As this description suggests, Twitter does allow people to feel a sense of identity and engagement, two key aspects of being a citizen.

TWITTER IN AMERICAN LIFE

We next turn to analyzing the population of Americans who use Twitter. Twitter is a social media platform that allows a user to send messages of up to 140 characters, as well as pictures, to the followers of that person or people who are tagged in the message.[1] A person can also use a hashtag—such as #GoUtes, for University of Utah items—that will allow people who look for certain hashtags to find stories of interest. Twitter now has more than two hundred million monthly active users worldwide, including 18% of all online Americans.[2] These users include ordinary citizens but also legislators, political parties, interest groups, and candidates. On Twitter, you can follow anyone else on the networks, from celebrities to athletes to news organizations to your friends. When they tweet, it shows up on your Twitter feed. According to Twitter's initial public offering (IPO) documents, in October 2013, there were approximately 49 million unique users in the United States, and its membership grows monthly.[3]

It is important to remember that Twitter is fundamentally different from Facebook and similar social networking websites. As William Oremus, slate.com's senior technology writer notes, a social networking site involves a reciprocal relationship; I am connected to friends and people I know on a social network site and we engage in a dialogue of sorts.[4] I can only "follow" people who agreed to be followed and, once this agreement occurs (i.e., they accept my friend request), we engage each other in some level of mutual communication. On Twitter, the relationship is much more of a nonreciprocal relationship. I follow LeBron James, NPR news, and the *New York Times* and read their tweets, but I have no expectation that LaBron is going to follow me or comment on my tweets. In part because Twitter accounts are public to anyone who looks, in part because of the structure of followers, and in part because of the character limit, Twitter is not viewed as a viable place for any kind of meaningful deliberative democracy and we do not examine it for evidence of political conversation. Rather, we are particularly interested in evaluating the quality of online political messages from elites. As Oremus writes,

> One Twitter user may be followed by millions of strangers whom she feels no obligation to follow back, any more than an evening news anchor feels the need to check in with each of her viewers every night at 6. As a media platform, Twitter's chief function is to help people keep up with what's going on in the world, and what influential people are thinking and doing at any given time. In that regard, it's closer to a news service than a social network.[5]

Studies of Twitter use reflect this nonreciprocal dynamic. Sysomos, a company that helps corporations evaluate the effectiveness of their social media presence, analyzed 11.5 million Twitter accounts in order to determine how this platform is used. There are several key findings to highlight as we think about Twitter in politics. They find that:

- 75% of Twitter activity is generated by just 5% of users, 91% is generated by 15% of users, and 97% is generated by the top 30% of users.
- On the other extreme, 85% of users post less than once per day and 21% have never Tweeted; not surprisingly, almost 64% of all Twitter users have fewer than 10 followers. Twitter users actually follow about the same number of people as they have followers up to 150 followers. After that point, people tend to follow more people than they have friends.
- Those who tweet frequently also tend to have many followers. Most people (85%) Tweet less than once a day.
- Those who have 800 followers (1.5% of Twitter users) tweet on average 3 times a day; those with 1,000 followers (0.42% of Twitter users) tweet 6 times per day, and those with 1,800 followers (1.1% of Twitter users) tweet 10 times per day on average.

These high users are not expecting a reciprocal communication and they are not even hoping to speak only to their followers. As Oremus notes,

Twitter's most influential users do not tweet with the expectation that they'll be heard only with the people who follow them directly. Rather, they treat the platform like it's a one-way TV interview, using Twitter to break news, to win arguments, to build their brands, to hone their public personas. That's because they understand that some of their tweets are likely to resonate far beyond Twitter.com and the Twitter app. The photo that Barack Obama tweeted when he won re-election was viewed by tens of millions of Americans who have never used Twitter.[6]

Twitter can be used to drive a news story or to attempt to move a story from the margins and make it more prominent, driving it into more mainstream media outlets. Obama's election photo is an example of a Tweet that "went viral" but also went mainstream and was picked up by traditional media outlets. The Colorado legislators who "blew up Twitter," discussed in chapter 2 of this book, were likely trying to accomplish something similar: driving a small interparty dispute into the mainstream media in order to achieve a political goal.

The Pew Research Center (2014) recently examined Twitter maps of conversations online and found that, on Twitter, partisans have very different conversations. They may talk about the same issues but they do not talk about the same issues in the same way. As one might expect, discussions of politics on Twitter occur within two distinct groups, "liberals and conservatives," that have little connectivity. This lack of connectivity means that, "Polarized Crowds on Twitter are not arguing. They are ignoring one another while pointing to different web resources and using different hashtags" (Pew 2014, 2). Liberals link to traditional news media and conservatives to alternate news stories, and each side communicates with people like them, not with people with diverse views.

When the federal government shutdown occurred in October 2013, both Republican and Democrats "Members and partisans in the public" were tweeting about the event, but they were not linking to the same articles, using the same hashtags, retweeting comments from the other side, or even commenting on articles from the other side. In short, the same event was occurring, but the two sides were not discussing the same event; their interpretations were different and occurring in separate parts of the "twitter-verse." For members of Congress, this means that Twitter may be a good tool for preaching to the converted. Yet the work of Pablo Barbera and colleagues (2015) finds significant evidence of cross-ideological engagement on Twitter and suggests previous work may have overestimated the degree of ideological segregation in social-media usage.

TWEETING DIRECTLY TO VOTERS

In examining how legislators use Twitters, we see evidence that legislators use it to communicate their ideological preferences directly to their constituents. There are various strategies that legislators can use with Twitter. Scholars have examined networks of Twitter followers, which allows them to estimate legislative ideology. Our analyses also show the relationship between the political content of the tweets of members of Congress and the district's preferences.

Barbera (2015) establishes policy positions of legislators by evaluating the links of Twitter users. In particular, he compares Twitter networks for members of the 112th Congress to estimates based on roll call votes. He writes, "the estimated ideal points are clustered into two different groups that align almost perfectly with party membership. The correlation between Twitter and roll-call-based ideal points is $\rho = .941$ in the House and $\rho = .0954$ in the Senate" (Barbera 2015, 82). This means that these two separate measurements have a mutual relationship where they fluctuate in the same directions at the same times—when one goes up, the other goes up, and when one goes down, the other goes down. It is important to note that this result comes from studying the network of Twitter users. It might seem that this network could potentially bias these findings, as the average American voter is unlikely to follow their representative on Twitter. Yet, other research by Justin Grimmer (2013) has established that, while legislators are aware that there is a small audience for their strategic communications, it is the case that the media and other interest groups will serve as amplifiers to the average citizen. In his landmark study on press releases and legislative communication styles, Grimmer finds that not only do legislators sincerely communicate about their ideologies in their public statements but also, moreover, moderates eschew policy debate, ensuring they can establish a broader base of support by communicating to claim credit instead. To confirm this result, though, we turn to another strategy to understand legislative tweeting.

We now focus on the second way to understand legislative Twitter strategies. Here, we rely on estimates of the ideological content of the tweets themselves as provided by Radford and Sinclair (2016). Relying on party identification and the content of the tweets, Radford and Sinclair (2016) estimate each legislator's Twitter ideology for the 112th Congress and provide a text-classifier for the words in the tweets that are useful in categorizing partisanship. Then, using that classifier, it is possible to establish which words in the tweets are nonpartisan. For our purposes in this chapter, we are particularly interested in two features of this work. First, we are interested in the relationship between estimated Twitter ideology and roll call voting ideology. The association between these estimates provides a real sense for whether legislators are tweeting in the same way as they are voting. We plot the Twitter ideology scores against the roll call voting scores in Figure 5.1.

In this figure, the x-axis describes the estimate of ideology using Twitter. The y-axis describes the estimate of ideology using roll call votes. The cluster in the lower left indicates the Democrats and the cluster in the upper right indicates the Republicans. We find that indeed there is a relatively strong association and that, in particular, we are able to easily discern the relationship between parties. Yet within-party associations are dramatically weaker. What could be driving the difference? We return to the notion that legislators will tweet a message that will reverberate to their district. We are particularly interested in knowing the relationship between those legislators who are misaligned and those who are

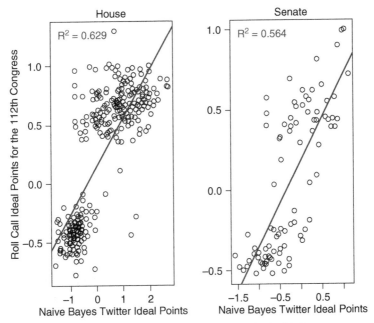

Figure 5.1 Naive Bayes Comparison of Twitter and Roll Call Ideal Points

SOURCE: Hall, Radford and Sinclair, Twitter

using a high proportion of nonpartisan words. We reproduce the Radford and Sinclair (2016) figure here (Figure 5.2). To measure misalignment, we create a dichotomous variable that is coded one under two circumstances:

- When a district is represented by a Democratic member of Congress, and in the most recent presidential election the Democratic presidential candidate received less than the national vote share (51%) of the vote in that district.
- When a district is represented by a Republican member of Congress, and in the most recent presidential election the Republican presidential candidate received less than the national vote share (49%) of the vote in that district.

Now we are particularly interested in how a legislator will tweet when he or she is misaligned from their district. In a linear regression where we predict the proportion of nonpartisan tweets, we would then say that there is a statistically significant increase in nonpartisan tweeting associated with misalignment, and that misalignment would be associated with a nearly 17% increase in nonpartisan tweeting.

Figure 5.2 describes, in essence, what legislative social media is accomplishing. When legislators are misaligned with their districts, they tweet nonpartisan messages. Voters listen. We don't know much about the content of these messages without further systematic study. A quick look at some of them, though, reveals that the nonpartisan language has a great deal to do with the district.

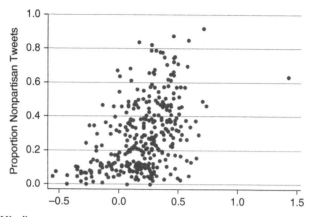

Figure 5.2 Misalignment
SOURCE: Hall, Radford and Sinclair, Twitter

For example, a tweet from Marco Rubio says, "Meets with Cuban exiles at summit—reinforces importance of democracy in western hemisphere." We suggest this kind of interaction is evidence of legislator's building trust, a kind of district "homestyle," as described by Richard Fenno. After careful observation ("soaking and poking"), Fenno (1978) concludes that members of Congress will wage more successful re-election campaigns by cultivating personal relationships with their districts (homestyle). If we conceptualize Twitter as a public record of direct communication between representatives and constituents, then this record of "homestyle" is increasingly available via social media and is particularly visible via Twitter. We believe that constituents would indeed benefit from this kind of direct communication, so by evaluating the political content of the tweets of members of Congress we are able to evaluate the extent to which legislators are speaking directly to their districts. While there is a tension between communicating an ideological message versus a "homestyle" message, we see that the legislators who would most benefit from speaking directly to their districts— those legislators who are misaligned—are in fact engaged in delivering nonpartisan Tweets. There is a long-standing belief in political science that voters reward homestyle (presentation of self, Fenno 2013). Homestyle can be characterized by a combination of district-specific communication combined with district-specific interest—"If people like you and trust you as an individual, they will vote for you" (Fenno 1978, 55–56). This preference allows the paradox to develop where "Americans hate Congress, but love their congressperson" (Fenno 1978). What better to capture this then Rubio tweeting to his district about Cuban exiles?

What have we learned about legislative tweets? We know that legislators tweet something similar to their party identification, broadly construed. Moreover, we know that deviations from their strategy of tweeting something similar to their partisanship occur only when their district is misaligned, suggesting that legislators are highly *strategic* about the messages they communicate to their constituents.

THE TWEETING PRESIDENT

There has not been extensive scholarly research on the use of Twitter by the president of the United States. President Obama created a Twitter account in 2007, but his tweets were often sent by members of his communication staff or by staff at Organizing for Action (OFA), which was a not-for-profit organization created to advocate for Obama's agenda.[7] Tweets signed "BO" from the @BarackObama account were from President Obama, and tweets from @POTUS or @WhiteHouse were sent from his communications staff. The presidency of Donald Trump changed all of this. President Trump used his Twitter handle @realDonaldTrump to tweet extensively during the presidential campaign and continues to do so as president. Although the White House continues to have the @WhiteHouse and @POTUS twitter handles—they were handed over seamlessly on January 20, 2017—it is the president's personal Twitter handle that is most often followed.

President Trump's use of Twitter is unprecedented in many ways. The President has used his personal Twitter account to make official policy statements, such as the announcement that Christopher Wray was being nominated to be the head of the FBI. In the case of the Wray nomination, it was not just the public that found out about the nomination on Twitter; members of Congress found out this way, as well as members his own staff.[8]

The *Los Angeles Times* noted, "The use of Twitter to make the high-profile announcement solidified the social media tool's role as Trump's primary mode of public communication, despite some concern from fellow Republicans. Trump insisted defiantly this week that Twitter remains his best tool to deliver unfiltered news to his supporters."[9] The use of Twitter by Trump led presidential spokesperson Sean Spicer to say:

> The president is the president of the United States so they're considered official statements by the president of the United States. The president is the most effective messenger on his agenda, and I think his use of social media—he now has a collective total of close to 110 million people across different platforms—gives him an opportunity to speak directly to the American people, which has proved to be a very effective tool? The same people who are critiquing his use of it now critiqued it during the election, and it turned out pretty well for him then.

During his first months in office, President Trump used Twitter to make foreign policy comments related to trade, NATO, terrorist attacks in London and Paris, and a variety of other topics. He also used Twitter to make comments about judges, his proposed travel ban, and a variety of other policy topics. Some of his most controversial tweets were related to the firing of FBI Director James Comey and the investigation of Russian involvement in the 2016 election. All of these tweets allowed the president to communicate directly to a larger public and to more specific individuals as well.

One thing that is important to understand about how candidate Trump engaged and President Trump engages Twitter is that Twitter provides him a mechanism to attract free traditional media. According to the media-tracking firm mediaQuant, candidate Trump received $4.96 billion in free media in 2016, which was more free media than was generated by Hillary Clinton, Bernie Sanders, Ted Cruz, Paul Ryan and Marco Rubio combined.[10] When Trump tweets early in the morning, he often can set the media agenda for the rest of the day. During the campaign, his tweets would lead to requests for interviews on cable news shows and national and local stations as well (ABC, CBS, Fox, and NBC, and their local affiliates). Twitter provided candidate Trump with a way to use new media to then dominate the narrative in traditional media and to get traditional media to amplify his messages. This use of new media to dominate traditional media was one of the important lessons from the Trump campaign.

Tweets That Connect

Recent research shows one reason why Trump has been such a successful user of Twitter. He understands how to use language effectively and appeal to people's moral emotions. Moral emotions require a high degree of self-reflection and include very powerful emotions. One especially powerful set of moral emotions, called "other-condemning" emotions, include contempt, anger, and disgust. These emotions are so powerful because they "motivate people to change their relationships with moral violators" (Haidt 2003, 854). These emotions and the desire to act based on these emotions can be triggered easily, even by watching movies or reading fictionalized accounts.

Part of the power of these emotions is that they can serve to create a strong social bond among like-minded people and create an "other" that is the target of the emotion. A simple example is racism. In the Jim Crow South, some whites would hold blacks in contempt or feel disgusted by the idea of sharing amenities (drinking fountains, restrooms, schools) with them. This would create a strong bond with other members of the in-group (whites like them) and a strong opposition to the out-group (blacks). These other-condemning emotions tend to trigger action— a desire to rectify a violation of a moral order—and also trigger group bonding. When people think "others" (the "out-group") are violating the moral order, people often react by becoming more strongly linked to people like them (the "in-group").

Brady et al. (2017) examined the use of emotional language in online communications, focusing on two classes of emotions: moral emotions and nonmoral emotions. Moral emotions are expressed through words like "attack," "bad," "blame," "are," "destroy," "fight," "hate," or "shame." Examples of nonmoral emotion words are "agree," "challenge," "lost," "support," "truth," and "worry." The linkage between morality and emotions is strong: emotions typically are strongly linked to and serve to amplify moral judgments. Brady et al. (2017, 1) note, "compared with nonmoral emotions, moral emotions are those that are most often associated with societal norms and are elicited by interests that may go beyond self-interest." Importantly, moral emotions may also be tied specifically to behavior that is relevant to morality and politics, including judgments of responsibility and voting. "Because moral-emotional language taps into our emotions deeply, its use in online communications should increase the likelihood that information will go viral."

Examining three polarized policy issues—gun control, same-sex marriage, and climate change—discussed on Twitter, Brady et al. tested whether using moral-emotional language would increase the overall diffusion of a tweet. They also tested whether moral-emotional language increased the diffusion of a tweet within ideological groups (did a conservative tweet get retweeted more within conservative circles) and across ideological groups (did liberals retweet the conservative tweet too). Not surprisingly, they found that messages that made the greatest use of moral-emotional language also were retweeted the most. (They controlled for the use of distinctly moral or distinctly emotional words). One key point the authors make is that there is a difference between communicating using emotional language and communicating moral-emotional language. Emotion is important, but language that is moral-emotional results in a distinct form of contagion.

They also found that the positive or negative bias of the emotional language influenced whether a tweet went viral. For example, when discussing same-sex marriage, positive moral-emotional language was retweeted more than negative emotional language, but the reverse was the case for climate change. So expressions of anger lowered the likelihood that a same-sex marriage tweet would be retweeted but increased the likelihood that a climate change tweet would be retweeted. And if you want your tweet to languish, tweet sadness; across all three topics, tweets that were associated with sadness had a decreased likelihood of being retweeted.

Moral-emotional language also tends to bring members of a group together. Tweets that had strong moral-emotional language were more likely to spread within an ideological group network (among liberals or among conservatives) compared to across networks (from conservative to liberal or vice versa). Tweets containing moral-emotional language were also communicated more within a network than were tweets containing nonmoral language. In short, people are more activated by moral emotional language, especially when it is framed correctly "positively or negatively, based on the topic in question" but people are most likely to hear that message only if they share the same ideology as the person who tweeted it.

TWITTER BOTS, POPULARITY, AND FAKE NEWS (PART 1)

There is a famous cartoon from *The New Yorker* that shows two dogs talking, with one of them sitting in front of a computer. The dog in front of the computer says to the other one, "On the Internet, nobody knows you're a dog." The point of the cartoon is simple yet profound; it is often impossible to know whether a person online is who they say they are, or even whether they are a person at all. On Twitter, there are real people—often people with verified accounts that have a blue check mark next to their Twitter handle—and there are bots. Rob Dubbin explained Twitter bots quite effectively in *The New Yorker*:[11]

> Twitter bots are, essentially, computer programs that tweet of their own accord. While people access Twitter through its Web site and other clients, bots connect directly to the Twitter mainline, parsing the information in real time and post- ing at will; it's a code-to-code connection, made possible by Twitter's wide-open application programming interface, or A.P.I. The bots, whose DNA can be writ- ten in nearly any modern programming language, live on cloud servers, which never go dark and grow cheaper by the day. This broad accessibility, magnified by Twitter's laudably permissive stance on the creation of new accounts, has created fertile ground for . . . automated shenanigans.

An individual can create his or her own bots to do what they want, or a person can purchase Twitter bots and Twitter followers. In an interview with *GQ* magazine, the comedian Joe Mande discussed how he buys friends Twitter followers as presents and also purchased them for his own Twitter account.[12] Gilad Lotan, the chief data scientist at Betaworks, discussed what happened when he purchased 4,000 Twitter followers. He found that the bots he pur- chased were following many other people who looked like buyers as well— politicians, entertainers, and corporations who want to look more legitimate and popular online. Most importantly, he found that his purchase of bots increased his overall ranking on search engines like Bing and his status on systems that measure online social influence metrics. Over time, the fake fol- lowers also led to him having more followers—real and bots—in the months that followed.[13]

Scholars at Oxford University's Oxford Internet Institute (OII) examined the impact of Twitter bots on the 2016 election and found that the bots had a profound impact in several areas. First, Twitter bots were effective in amplifying the messages of candidates. For example, after the first presidential debate, "more than four times as many tweets were made by automated accounts in favour of Donald Trump around the first US presidential debate as by those backing Hillary Clinton."[14] The preponderance of fake accounts, and their growing role in politics, has been documented by *Newsweek*, which claims as of 2017 that nearly half of Donald Trump's Twitter followers are fake accounts and bots, compared to 2016, where only 8% were fake accounts and bots. To put this in comparison, as of 2017, 79% of President Obama's followers were real.[15] This is not to claim that the Trump campaign itself was behind this activity; the study by the OII did not examine the people behind the bots, only that they existed. It is also important to note that, even without the bots, there were more than twice as many pro-Trump tweets as pro-Clinton tweets after the first debate. The OII ex- amined the number of tweets posted the last week of the election—November 1 and November 9—and found that "Twitter bots accounted for nearly a quarter of all postings that included hashtags related to the election . . . proTrump hashtags got five times as much traffic from automated accounts as hashtags that were pro- Hillary Clinton."[16] The researchers noted that content from these bots declined precipitously after the 2016 election, suggesting that the bots had served their purpose for the election and were no longer being deployed.

Second, Twitter bots can be used to spread fake news. For example, in the weeks leading up to the 2016 election, there were stories claiming that an FBI agent connected to Hillary Clinton's email disclosures had murdered his wife and shot himself, voting would be postponed until Thursday, Democrat voters could text their vote in to their local election office, and that Hillary Clinton had a stroke over the weekend.[17] Since the election, social media have been used to spread fake news targeting liberals. As Vox noted, there is a growing network of claims surrounding President Trump and Russia that feed into the belief among many on the left that there must have been concerted collaboration between the Trump campaign and the Russian government. As Vox notes, there is not one singular unified theory that shapes these theories; instead there are a wide range of theories floating about online that are unfounded but fit into a worldview that some people have regarding Russia and the Trump campaign.[18]

The OII researchers also collected data on news sharing by people in the state of Michigan using political twitter hashtags. What they found was that there was quite a bit of political sharing going on by the people studied but the quality of what was shared was rather low. Specifically, people generally were not sharing news from the mainstream media or well-researched information. Instead people were sharing "extremist, sensationalist, conspiratorial, masked commentary, fake news and other forms of junk news" and the sharing of mainstream news and well-researched information declined steadily over the course of the last weeks of the election.[19] Former FBI agent Clint Watts testified before the US Senate Intelligence Committee about how various Russian actors used Twitter bots to spread fake news during the 2016 election. These Twitter bots were created carefully, with Russians identifying key characteristics of Trump supporters—conservative, white, Christian—and ensuring that all of the information and photos used on the Twitter accounts would make the bots "look" like their target audience: Trump voters. Watts testified, "whenever you're trying to socially engineer [American voters] and convince them that the information [being shared online] is true, it's much more simple because you see somebody and they look exactly like you, even down to the pictures."[20] The New York Times did a case study of how fake news spreads. The story started with a photo of charter buses and a person's claim that the buses were being used to bring paid protesters to a Trump rally in Texas. His initial post included three photos of charter buses and the words: "Anti-Trump protestors in Austin today are not as organic as they seem. Here are the busses they came in. #fakeprotests #trump2016 #austin."[21] Because of his use of several popular hashtags, the tweets were noticed by people, and the tweet and information were posted on a conservative forum on the website Reddit. From here, the post was picked up by a conservative discussion forum, and from there the tweet became part of a broader news discussion, as it was picked up by bloggers, various Facebook pages, and ultimately mainstream media companies worked to verify the story. Ironically, the person who posted the information realized that the post was false after several days and removed the tweet. However, by then, the story was circulating throughout the twitterverse.

THE PSYCHOLOGY OF FAKE NEWS

For psychologists, the reason why fake news is so attractive to people is easy to understand. It falls at the intersection of several biases people generally have and heuristics that people use. For many people, these biases are reinforced by the political ideologies that they hold. Key biases that people have are implicit bias and confirmation bias.[22]

The first bias people bring to the world of the Internet is implicit bias. Implicit bias is a form of stereotyping; it is categorizing and grouping people for the purpose of determining who is part of the in-group (people who are like us) and out-group (people not like us). If you think Asians are good at math, this is your brain on implicit bias! Implicit bias has been very helpful historically; people in the out-group often wanted to kill you or were less trustworthy. Today, this bias tends to lead to viewing things uncritically if someone who is part of our in-group presents it to us. Online, implicit bias is problematic because we often take information presented to us by our in-group at face value. If you are conservative and Breitbart or Rush Limbaugh or Fox News presents something to you, you take it at face value and don't feel the need to vet the information to determine whether it is actually true. Likewise, liberals are just as likely to take things presented to them on MSNBC, on Daily Kos, or Slate.com at face value.

The second bias we have is confirmation bias. People seek out information that confirms their existing beliefs. If you think global warming exists and I present you with information that global warming is a problem, you drink up that information. However, the flip side is that when we are presented with information that challenges our biases, we tend to discount it. For example, if you think autism is caused by vaccinations, then you will discount research that shows vaccinations are safe. Confirmation bias can actually become quite pernicious because it can lead to people doubling down on their initial beliefs. If you think climate change is a hoax or that vaccines cause autism, the more information I present to you showing you are wrong, the more likely you may be to double down on your initial beliefs.

A third bias that people have is referred to as naive realism. This is the idea that we view ourselves as objective viewers of the world. We know the truth and people who do not agree with us must be dumb, biased, or ill-informed. We often think we understand things even though we do not actually understand the underlying science. For example, psychologists at Yale asked graduate students if they understood how a zipper, a toilet, and a cylinder lock worked. The students all said they understood how each work. However, when asked to write a detailed description of how each worked, the students realized their knowledge was rather limited. We think we understand things because we are told others understand them and we take at face value that this information is accurate.

Fourth, there is the idea of a bias blind spot. Quite simply, we think that other people have biases but we do not! Imagine I ask you to explain to me why current US immigration policy is either good or bad. If you are a liberal, you may search for articles from *Mother Jones* and *The Nation* and if you are a conservative, you might look at articles in *National Review* and *The Weekly Standard*. In both cases, you have searched for articles that are in biased sources, these magazines have known slants, yet you will perceive that your analysis is impartial and objective and you will present it that way to others.

Together, these biases work to create serious problems in the online world. We think we know things we do not really know. We seek out information that confirms our biases. We take at face value what people like us say, and we think we are models of objectivity (but that people who do not agree with us are a bit dim)! With these ideas in mind, it is easy to see how fake news proliferates. Fake news is designed to play on these biases, and Twitter, which is designed for small snacks of information, is a perfect medium for spreading this type of news. We glance at our phone while waiting for something, and there it is, a story that fits our biases and worldview. If we do not take the time to use www.snopes.com or a similar fact-checking website when we read a story that seems almost too good to be true and is not being widely reported elsewhere, we may fall victim of fake news.

THE TWITTERVERSE AND AMERICAN POLITICS

In this chapter, we have focused on the role that Twitter plays in connecting legislators to voters and also considered some of the problems associated with Twitter generally. The ability of politicians to communicate directly with the public is one of the great benefits of new media, but eliminating the mainstream media from the process has several risks. The mainstream media are designed to filter political messages and place the claims of politicians into a context. For example, mainstream media have the capacity to inform the public if a politician is tweeting a message that is different from their vote choice or is trying to obscure their true ideological position. As was noted earlier, many voters do not have the appropriate levels of political knowledge and sophistication to place a politician's claim in the correct political or policy context. Nonetheless, Twitter does allow for increased transparency and increased engagement; a legislator can speak directly to you and you can reply directly to them.

In the analyses in this chapter, we observe a significant association between a legislator's party identification and their Twitter speech. We also observed that legislators who are ideologically misaligned from their district are much more likely to engage in nonpartisan speech. These are normatively positive attributes of having legislators feel accountable to their constituents, and we observe constraints on the legislators' speech that is associated with district preferences. Moreover, given that legislators are speaking directly to their constituents, it is generally a good thing that legislators are communicating sincerely about their partisanship and to some extent to their roll call voting patterns.

The complicating factor of this direct communication is that voters tend to amplify the messages when they communicate to each other and do so within narrow partisan networks. Partisan speech is increasingly polarized: as Gentzkow et al. note, "America's two political parties speak different languages. Democrats talk about 'estate taxes', 'undocumented workers', and 'tax breaks for the wealthy', while Republicans refer to 'death taxes', 'illegal aliens', and 'tax reform'" (Gentzkow et al. 2016, 1). These authors find that the partisanship of language has become polarized to a state that has not been seen before. Because of the way in which Twitter works, the comments of partisans often are amplified within partisan spheres, with little cross-communication between Democrats and Republicans online.

If we consider the five questions posited in the preface, we can see that Twitter is an interesting form of social media. It is a very simple platform to access and use and, because it is designed for use on smartphones, is something that almost all Americans can access. However, relative to other social networks, Twitter is not as highly used by the general public. Twitter is an excellent source of information about politics because it is the go-to place for much of the media. It is often the first place where news is reported and people can get instant analysis of events from many of the most noted experts of elections and politics. All traditional media, from the *New York Times* to Fox News, are regularly posting new content on Twitter, and people can find links to longer articles via their Twitter feed. However, the positive aspects of Twitter—that it is an easy way for people to learn about politics and participate in political discussion—can be confounded by fake news. If people can avoid fake news, Twitter can be a positive source of information and discussion related to politics.

SUGGESTED READINGS

Fenno, Richard F. 1978. *Home Style: House Members in Their Districts* Longman Classics.

Barbera, Pablo. 2015. "Birds of the Same Feather Tweet Together: Bayesian Ideal Point Estimation Using Twitter Data." *Political Analysis* 23 (1): 76–91.

Grimmer, Justin. 2013. *Representational Style in Congress: What Legislators Say and Why It Matters.* Cambridge University Press.

CHAPTER 6

Discussing Politics
Face(book)-to-Face(book)

"If you agree, post this as your status for the rest of the day," reads a friend's Facebook status. Do you copy it and make it yours? Ideas spread across the world from one friend to another on the social network platform Facebook.

A **meme** is a humorous image that is copied, often with slight variations, and spread by Internet users. Memes provide one way that political information can be shared.

In March 2013, a red equals sign meme in support of marriage equality went "viral" on Facebook, resulting in 3 million Facebook users changing their profile picture to a red equals sign. What predicts this behavior? Two researchers examined the diffusion of the red equals sign and find that the diffusion of the meme across Facebook was best explained in that users would switch their profile picture after observing several of their friends doing so first (and this explanation transcends the typical social group membership traits of gender, age, education, and political ideology) (State and Adamic 2015). That is, the pattern of meme sharing (and of choosing a Facebook status) is largely driven by friendships.

This chapter illuminates the behavior of those individuals who share political information online. We find that the patterns of sharing we see online are largely supported by in-person behavior. The online sharing of politics mirrors the offline sharing of politics. While this is relatively encouraging news in terms of the capacity of people to be persuaded by a wave of false statements online, it also raises the question of how well people are insulated from a diverse set of views and how well they can acquire quality, truthful information. When we ask our survey respondents about the political information they find online, about half of them (52%) report that it is usually difficult to tell what is true from what is not true.

FACEBOOK AS A FORCE IN POLITICS

Before discussing how Facebook is used, it is helpful to understand why it is such a powerful platform. First, it is the largest new media platform in the world, with over 1.94 billion monthly active users in March 2017, including 1.15 billion mobile daily active users. Facebook is used more than Twitter, Instagram, and Whatsapp combined. Mobile Facebook use increased 23% from December 2015 to December 2016, which shows how mobile use is becoming the primary way in which new media are used. People use Facebook a lot—1.28 billion people logged onto Facebook at least daily in the first 3 months of 2017—and used the site for 20 minutes daily. Most people log into Facebook multiple times per day; in February 2017, the average person used the application 223 times during the month.[1] There are 510,000 comments posted, 293,000 statuses updated, and 136,000 photos uploaded every minute on Facebook.[2] Facebook and Facebook Messenger ranked first and second among the most popular mobile applications in the United States in 2016.[3]

In the political realm, Facebook is important because it has been linked to higher levels of civic engagement and political participation. Studies of college students have found that those who engage in even small types of political activity such as liking a candidate's page or posting a political post are more likely to engage in other forms of political activity. In addition, college students who are frequent users of Facebook have been shown to have somewhat higher levels of life satisfaction, social trust, civic engagement, and political participation. A Canadian study found that political Facebook participation led to other types of online and offline participation. The effects in these studies were small, which means that new media are not a cure-all for youth disengagement.[4]

Perhaps the most important study of the role of Facebook and politics is the 61-million-person experiment that was conducted by Robert Bond et al. during the 2010 congressional elections.[5] Given the work in political persuasion by Donald Green and Alan Gerber and others, which has found that face-to-face communication is one of the most effective means of political mobilization, a group of scholars set out to determine how effective communications spread through face-to-face social networks were. In 2010, they conducted a randomized controlled trial of political mobilization messages delivered to 61 million Facebook users. The study had three groups: first, a social message group, second, an informational message group, and third, a control group. The social message group received a message at the top of their News Feed encouraging them to vote and provided an information resource for finding their polling place. It also included three social messages: a clickable button reading "I Voted," a counter showing how many Facebook users had reported voting, and the profile pictures of six of the user's friends who had clicked the "I Voted" button. The informational message group received everything in the social group except for the faces of their friends who clicked "I Voted," and the control group received no voting message in their News Feed.

The study had two major findings. First, people who received the social message were more likely to vote compared to either the control group or the informational message group.[6] This suggests that just providing information to voters via Facebook is not a strong motivator for individuals to vote. Second, the authors found, "the messages not only influenced the users who received them but also the users friends, and friends of friends. The effect of social transmission on real-world voting was greater than the direct effect of the messages themselves, and nearly all the transmission occurred between close friends who were more likely to have a face-to-face relationship." The first finding is not completely unexpected. Providing people with a social message encourages them to vote. However, the second finding is incredibly important. What it means is that social messages not only affected the people targeted but also influenced the behavior of the person's friends. In fact, the effect on the person's friends was greater than the message itself. This study and others suggest that well-crafted messages that promote social messaging showing how a behavior is affecting a person's network well help the message spread through the social network. The authors note that social networks also help to reinforce transmissions of information through strong-tie networks, both online and offline.

The power of Facebook and how it affects people has been studied in other settings as well. In a rather famous study, scientists manipulated the types of posts people saw on their feeds, with some people seeing more positive messages and others seeing more negative ones. The study found that there was an emotional contagion; people who saw less positive emotional content also posted less positive information and people who saw less negative emotional content also posted less negative content. The study concluded that emotions expressed by friends, via online social networks, influence our own moods, constituting, to our knowledge, the first experimental evidence for massive-scale emotional contagion via social networks. This study again illustrates the power of Facebook in transmitting information that can affect our emotional state. Given the role that emotions play in politics, it is clear how important Facebook is to the American political scene.[7]

CONTENT OF SHARED MATERIAL

In 2012 we asked a nationally representative sample of survey respondents a series of questions about the ways in which they both obtain and share political information online.[8] First, let's take a look at how a typical American obtains online information. The first column of Table 6.1 shows the percentage of our survey respondents who reported obtaining political information from that source in the last two days.

We find that most people obtain their online political information from very traditional sources. The source that occurs most frequently is direct campaign contact via email—an email from a campaign, candidate, or political organization (43%). Next people turn to websites from traditional media (newspapers,

Table 6.1 Political Information Source (in the last two days)

INFORMATION SOURCE	PERCENTAGE	FORWARDED	POSTED	TWEETED	TALKED
Email from campaign	43.1	9.28	4.41	1.39	10.21
Website from news source	41.4	7	10.39	1.69	14.73
Email from friend/family	34.5	19.42	5.22	0.58	11.88
Website of campaign	27.1	12.92	9.23	1.85	18.45
Person on a SNS	23.7	5.06	10.13	2.53	10.97
Organization on a SNS	20.1	9.45	32.84	2.99	25.87
Blog about politics	17.7	11.30	18.64	3.95	29.94
YouTube	13.5	6.67	7.41	3.70	8.89
Twitter	7.3	1.37	8.22	17.81	23.29

NOTE: The column percentage shared reflect the percentage of individuals who responded out of the total who had obtained political information from the row source.

Source: Hall and Sinclair

magazines, or TV station websites) (41%), and then to direct personal contact via email—an email from a family, friend, or coworker (34%). Finally, 27% of people report using a campaign, candidate, or political organization website. That is, these online sources are not so different from the traditional ways in which people have obtained political information—from campaigns, from traditional media, and from their social environment. Modern social media—social networking sites–do play a role as well. People reported using social networking sites to get information, either from a political organization (20 percent) or a person (23 percent). Least common were the most novel of new media: a mere 7% of respondents reported using Twitter to get political information, 17% reported using a blog, and 13% reported using YouTube. To summarize, the profile of the typical online American's political information sources is not so different from what we would imagine without the availability of these resources online. Yet, the principle difference that arises is with respect to the fact that this information can now be shared, from one person to another. We then asked our respondents for each of the sources described above, what did they do with the information? The columns in Table 6.1 reflect the percentage of individuals who report sharing their political information. Two big points emerge from this table. First, regardless of the online political information source, people are very likely to talk to others about what they find online. Indeed, across all sources of information there are only two instances where people are more likely to share information via other online media than they are to talk to each other. Second, there is an indication that media are unlikely to travel from one channel to another. That is, if you get an email from a friend or family member, you are more likely to forward it (via email) than you are to post it on a social networking site (19% of people forwarded the email, compared to 5% of people who posted). Similarly, if you get information from a political organization on a social networking site, you are more likely to post information to a social networking site than you are to forward an email (32% vs. 9%, respectively). The same is true with Twitter: getting information via Twitter (which happens somewhat rarely) implies you are most likely to retweet the information (17% vs. 1% for email forwarding and 8% for social networking site posting).

This question matters because shared material is increasingly constituting a larger share of an individual's news diet; news that is reported from less conventional news sources constitutes a larger portion of what is shared online and additionally than what is indirectly covered by more central news. As reported in 2017,

> According to the report from Harvard's Berkman Klein Center for Internet & Society, which applied data analysis techniques to 2 million election stories to understand better what people were reading and sharing, Trump not only got the most attention from media outlets across the political spectrum, but his preferred core issues—immigration, jobs and trade—received significant coverage and were widely shared online. In contrast, news about Clinton focused negatively on her family charitable foundation, her use of a private email server as U.S. secretary of state, and the 2012 terrorist attack in Benghazi, Libya, the study found.
>
> Surprisingly, while "center-left" mainstream news organizations such as The New York Times and CNN remained popular and influential news sources, far-right upstarts such as Breitbart and Daily Caller, and even hoax-peddling sites such as Gateway Pundit, were able to drive mainstream election news coverage and dominate social media sharing of election news with far greater power and effectiveness than previously understood, the researchers found.[9]

In a world where Breitbart dominates the national conversation and the *Wall Street Journal* doesn't, we increasingly care about the structure of online sharing. Sharing is playing this new role in the new media revolution. Who is doing the sharing?

WHO ARE THE CONNECTORS?

If we divide our population of survey respondents into two types of people, we could consider some people to be *sharers*, individuals who are willing to share information online, and other people to be *talkers*, individuals who are willing to talk about political information to each other. In our survey, we have about 15% of the respondents who report they are a *talker*, while about 17% of the respondents report they are a sharer. About 8% of people report being both a *talker* and a *sharer*. But, let's focus on whether there are differences between those people who are only talkers or sharers. We look at gender, age, education, race, voter registration status, party identification, and media use. Remarkably, there are almost no significant differences between talkers and sharers. Sharers are a little bit older, but otherwise their profiles are similar. That is, the connectors *online* are extremely similar to the connectors *offline*. What is unique, then, about the role of online political information is that it can move from an online platform into a personal conversation. Yet, the online world is not particularly isolated from personal interactions. Interestingly, our respondents do prefer to share information with others in a more passive way. When we asked individuals whether they had engaged in sharing political information across a variety of strategies, they were much more likely to report they had shared links, photos, or clicked a "like" button than they were to report that they had directly encouraged others to vote or donate or even electronically shared information via a tweet, post, email, or online forum. That is, just over 46% of our respondents were willing to engage in some kind of "slacktivism," whereas a more aggressive kind of sharing engendered only 28% participation. Additionally, very few people report engaging in political deliberation. When asked how a typical respondent would act after a friend posted something on a social networking site that she disagreed with, only 17% said they would post a comment and a mere .69% claimed they would post something of their own. Almost half of our respondents (just over 47%) said they would simply ignore the post.

TWO-STEP FLOW: THE POTENTIAL MAGNITUDE OF SHARING POLITICS THROUGH NEW MEDIA

When we ask our survey respondents about the political information they find online, about half of them (52%) report that it is usually difficult to tell what is true from what is not true. The myriad of possibilities for blogs, news reports, and references that espouse false information makes it very challenging for a typical citizen to parse through political content. That is, even though there is more accessible political information now than ever before, people need help parsing through the content. That is, people rely on the connectors—those individuals who parse through political content and are trusted personal resources.

To demonstrate this point, we asked people to rank the sources by which they obtained useful political information. One caveat with this type of question is that people may forget, causing them to accidently misreport, or they may deliberately lie, wanting to appear more politically sophisticated. In most studies of political participation we focus on data where we are able to directly observe the participation choices instead of relying on the individuals to self-report their political behaviors. This is because we know that, for example, survey respondents tend to over-report particular decisions that are socially desirable, like the decision to turn out to vote in an election.[10] Indeed, they may not even be aware of the source that was the catalyst for their political opinion. Yet, to the extent people can correctly recall their sources, we find that people report relying on very traditional sources in forming opinions or deciding for whom to vote. In particular, people report relying on local and national televised news and newspapers (either online or in print) most frequently. Next come the connectors: people report direct conversations with friends, family, and coworkers as the third-ranked source. Radio, surprisingly, comes fourth. Then fifth and sixth are email from friends, family, and coworkers, followed by posts from family, friends, and coworkers on social networking sites. Finally are the contacts by campaigns or candidates themselves (candidate websites, candidate emails, and political advertisements). Last are blogs and Twitter.

SHARED MEMES

We gave our respondents a set of memes and asked them what they would do if they had seen such an image circulating on the web. These images are displayed in Figure 6.1. We tried to vary the content of these images: in one, we have a funny cat picture. The four others are all political, two positive (one for Obama and one for Romney) and two negative. In each meme, someone has added text to a picture to make a political point.

In particular we are interested in whether people are more likely to share things that are positive; we would also imagine they would be more likely to share things that are funny (like the cat meme). In general, the pattern of sharing for these memes is described in Table 6.2.

Figure 6.1 Meme Images
Imgur bMpGK; Flickr/Dateschwanz; The Red State Report; Memegenerator/Mitt Romney Meme; Able2Know/RapRap

Table 6.2 Shared Memes

MEME	READ	FORWARD VIA EMAIL	POST TO SOCIAL MEDIA	TALK ABOUT WITH FRIENDS
Kitten	28.08	5.92	4.21	5.52
Positive Obama	21.20	4.90	4.90	14.70
Negative Obama	16.53	4.91	3.01	11.92
Positive Romney	19.72	2.70	2.90	14.31
Negative Romney	16.95	3.81	3.91	15.55

Source: Hall and Sinclair

As we might have expected, looking at the first column of Table 6.2, we see that the kitten meme is most highly read (28%), followed by the positive memes (21% for the positive Obama meme and 20% for the positive Romney meme). The negative memes are much less likely to be read, with only close to 17% readership for each. If this set of memes says anything in general about the pattern of meme sharing, it suggests that negativity is not necessarily rewarded. The most interesting thing about memes is the degree to which they are shared. Thus we want to compare the rate at which these memes are either posted to social media or inhabit actual conversations with friends. For example, while the kitten meme is posted at similar rates to the other memes, it is seldom the point of social conversation. Instead, the negative Romney meme has the greatest rate of conversation, followed by the positive Romney and positive Obama meme. What is most interesting about this data is the extent to which people are reporting that they are *much* more likely to have conversations about what they see online then they are to share online political information.

ONLINE SHARING OCCURS LESS FREQUENTLY THAN ACTUAL POLITICAL CONVERSATIONS

Sharing political memes is a specific kind of political participation with two implications. First, simply by sharing politics across a new media platform it is the case that many more people can be exposed to an idea quickly. Second, people are highly influenced by the political behavior of their friends, typically because of a desire to adhere to a common norm of behavior (Sinclair 2012). In some of the earliest research on social movements, Doug McAdam (1986) found that college students' volunteer participation in the Freedom Summer voter registration drive was largely driven by friendship ties. This was extremely politically costly political participation, entailing real risk of political harm. If the Freedom Summer students could be driven to participate based on friendship ties, then surely Facebook users can be compelled to share memes based on similar relationships.

Yet, many have claimed that the online sharing of political information is relatively costless (and indeed we observe that many individuals prefer online sharing that is closer to slacktivism than activism). Is it the case, then, that meme sharing has little influence on the political process?

In this chapter we argue that indeed it does, for two reasons. First, it is challenging for people to ascertain what is true online. Consequently they deeply rely on their friendship networks to sort out complicated political information. Second, we note that by examining a survey where we inquire not only about online behavior but also about offline political conversations, we are able to discover that indeed offline political conversations occur at greater regularity, and furthermore that those individuals who are sharing online only have socio-economic, political, and demographic profiles that are similar to those individuals to are sharing via conversation alone.

FAKE NEWS (PART 2)

Which of these do you think is a real story? First, "Obama Signs Executive Order Banning the Pledge of Allegiance in Schools Nationwide." Second, "Pope Francis Shocks World, Endorses Donald Trump for President, Releases Statement." Third, "Colorado Cops Search for Poop-and-Run Jogger." If you answered item number three, you are correct![11] How certain were you of your answer? How hard is it for you to ascertain fact from fiction?

As we discussed in chapter 5, fake news was a major issue in the 2016 election and Facebook was affected by this phenomenon. The problem of fake news on Facebook was brought to the fore by a study by Buzzfeed, which found that

> the top-performing fake election news stories on Facebook generated more engagement than the top stories from major news outlets such as the *New York Times*, *Washington Post*, Huffington Post, NBC News, and others. . . .
>
> During [the final three] months of the campaign, 20 top-performing false election stories from hoax sites and hyperpartisan blogs generated 8,711,000 shares, reactions, and comments on Facebook.
>
> Within the same time period, the 20 best-performing election stories from 19 major news websites generated a total of 7,367,000 shares, reactions, and comments on Facebook.[12]

There were approximately four times as many positive but fake pro-Trump stories shared on Facebook as compared to positive but fake pro-Clinton stories.

The proliferation of fake news, and the fact that it outperformed real news during the last three months of the campaign, is troubling. In 2016 alone, "fake news about US politics accounted for 10.6 million of the 21.5 million total shares, reactions, and comments these English-language stories generated on Facebook."[13] However, there are conflicting views about whether seeing fake news has an impact on voters. One set of researchers at New York University and Stanford University found that fake news stories on Facebook in 2016 were only read by approximately 15% of voters. Whether or not people believed the stories they saw was affected by the person's ideological leanings. People who were strong partisans were approximately 15% more likely to believe articles that aligned with their ideological preferences, and bias was stronger for individuals who are part of single-ideology social networks. This study suggested that it was unlikely that seeing one or two fake news articles would have shifted people's attitudes and vote choice in the election.[14]

Researchers at Yale University found that the power of fake news comes from this familiarity. Because the stories often fit into our own narrative, people are willing to believe fake news. The Yale study is disturbing because it suggests that fake news persists in our memories and is hard to debunk. The study concludes:

> Not only were more familiar fake news headlines rated as more accurate, but a single exposure to fake news headlines was sufficient to measurably increase perceptions of their accuracy. Moreover, this effect increased with a second exposure, which suggests a compounding effect of familiarity across time. Explicitly warning individuals that the fake news headlines have been disputed by third-party fact-checkers (which was true in every case) did not abolish or even significantly diminish this effect. **That is, becoming familiar with a fake news story by learning that it was disputed led to higher accuracy judgments compared to previously unfamiliar fake news stories.**[15]

It is troubling that one exposure to a fake story can influence a person's beliefs. What is more troubling is that attempting to prove the story is false leads people to double down and *really believe* the story is true. Just being warned that a story is not true does not inoculate a person from believing the falsehood and a false story becomes more and more powerful with repetition.

A study of high school students from across the United States illustrates one problem with debunking fake news, which is that many of them cannot tell a real news source apart from a fake one when each is presented to them on Facebook. The problems identified in this study were multifold. First, people did not know how to verify whether a news account or person's account is real or not. Second, they did not know the difference between news items and sponsored content, and why the sponsored content might not be as accurate or appropriate. Third, people did not give much thought to using Google or other searches to determine whether something that seemed dubious was actually true. Together, these items mean that people often are not taking the time to verify the accuracy of information they see on Facebook.[16]

The issue of verifying news led Facebook to create a fact-checking process after the 2016 election. Specifically, articles can be flagged as questionable by Facebook users and the article will be given to a third-party fact checker like Snopes.com. The fact checker will then either flag the item as questionable or say it is correct and fact checked. Articles that are flagged will be flagged throughout Facebook, and when a person attempts to share such a story, the person will be prompted as to whether they want to share a questionable article.[17] Unfortunately, the research literature suggests that people do not pay attention to warnings that information is fake and instead read things that fit into their own biases.

MEMES, INFORMATION, AND CONVERSATION: POLITICAL CONVERSATION BETWEEN PEOPLE STILL DOMINATES NEW MEDIA

First, take a moment to realize that not all news sources are truthful. Second, take a moment to realize that not everyone can discern fact from fiction. Indeed, 52% of our respondents report finding it challenging to discern truth from fiction online. Fake news websites have sprung up all over the Internet, spewing claims like the pope endorsing Donald Trump or Donald Trump pulling ahead of Hillary Clinton in the popular vote.[18] As the *New York Times* explains, in the last three months of the US presidential campaign, the top 20 fake news stories generated more engagement (likes, shares, etc.) on Facebook than the top 20 truthful news stories. Facebook is a critical source for news. According to a recent Pew Research Center report on social media (2014), "Facebook is now a widely-used source for news about government and politics. 39% of Americans get news from Facebook in a typical week." With growing concern in the social media community about fake news, what are the implications for the interaction of fake news and the new media revolution?

Recall that we found that in our experiment, the kitten meme is most highly read. That is, most people are not interested in politics. But, when we think about the impact of social sharing online, it isn't the kitten meme that generates the greatest rate of actual conversation—it is the negative Romney meme. This is important when we think about how people consume news, and why in particular they consume political news. People report relying on local and national televised news and newspapers (either online or in print) most frequently. Next come the connectors: people report direct conversations with friends, family, and coworkers as the third-ranked source. Regardless of the online political information source, people are very likely to talk to others about what they find online. In our analysis of what is shared, we find few instances where people are more likely to share information online than in conversations with each other. We conclude from these facts that while the majority of people do not seek out political information, when they do they may be exposed to false information, both directly from fake news sites and, of greater concern, from peers. People have relied on their friends, their connectors, to serve as filters for falsehoods. With the rise of fake news sites, and the challenge the connectors themselves find in discerning fact from fiction, it is increasingly likely that false information is penetrating the political networks of citizens and being distributed from one individual to another.

What can be done? We find two encouraging features. First, our respondents report that their shared media are unlikely to travel from one channel to another. That is, for example, if you get an email from a friend or family member, you are more likely to forward it (via email) than you are to post it on a social networking site. To the extent that false information circulates online, it seems to largely stay within the same channel. This is a way to contain false information or at least to hope that citizens can be exposed to multiple sources of information across different social media platforms, and that this exposure can generate a reasonable level of skepticism about what is true. The second encouragement is that social media companies are increasingly engaged in filtering out fake news. According to a Pew Research Center survey conducted in January 2016, 35% of respondents between ages 18 and 29 said that social media was the "most helpful" source of information about the presidential campaign (Gottfriend et al. 2016).

It is important to remember that Facebook is one of the most powerful tools for communicating news to Americans. Many Americans receive much of their news through their Facebook feed. Facebook also is a place where people can engage in discussions of political issues and have an incentive to be respectful in their discussions, since these are discussions with people they know. Because of its role as a communicator of news and information, Facebook encourages deliberation and also is a place where politicians can communicate with the public, both about their political and personal selves. On Facebook, your congresswoman can be both a politician and a person—a mother, a spouse, a friend, and a person who engages in popular culture. Facebook can humanize politics in ways that were not easily done in the days without new media.

Overall, the greatest opportunities for sharing come not from online conversations, but from in-person conversations. Online political engagement seems to be more passive, while actual deliberation may be more likely to happen in person.

SUGGESTED READINGS

Sinclair, Betsy. 2012. *The Social Citizen.* University of Chicago Press.

Prior, Markus. 2007. *Post-Broadcast Democracy: How Media Choice Increases Inequality in Political Involvement and Polarizes Elections.* Cambridge University Press.

Pew Research Center Report on Social Media, Political News and Ideology. 2014. http://www.journalism.org/2014/10/21/section-2-social-media-political-news-and-ideology

CHAPTER 7

Conclusion

This book presents a picture of what politics looks like for a connected public. By itself, no single chapter, anecdote, table, or figure provides the tableaux by which we can see what kind of citizenry emerges as a consequence of new media. Indeed, no single analysis could ever suffice. Even in an idealized context where there was a representative sample of American adults who were offline and to whom we could randomly assign Internet access, we would then need to further embed each of our subject's computers, phones, and houses with data collectors so that we could view the entirety of their new media exposures. Apart from the obvious violations of privacy, it would furthermore be simply impossible to analyze such data over a long enough time period to be meaningful or useful. Thus we are left with a fairly Herculean task as researchers: We need to find enough puzzle pieces to construct an image of what politics looks like for a population that heavily relies on new media. Each puzzle piece tells us something new, allowing us to triangulate toward a meaningful understanding about the role of new media in ordinary citizens' lives. In particular we want to understand to what extent new media allows people to be better citizens. In our conceptualization of citizenship, then, this means we are asking about the association between new media and shared identity, political knowledge, and political engagement. Social media changes the way in which people seek, receive, and share information, and we treat each component of this process as critical for democratic citizenship.

Our insights begin by establishing just who is online, and who not only has access to new media but also is willing to use it. We find strong evidence the digital divide is shrinking in terms of Internet access, but we do observe systematic differences with respect to age, income, and education. The digital divide exists in terms of race, with African Americans and Hispanics more likely to be offline than whites, but there are relatively minor differences in terms of gender. Encouragingly, that racial split is switched for social media, with Hispanics and African Americans more likely to be engaged in social media online. This may help to overcome historical differences in access. We see the rise in access as associated with reduced costs in terms of access, suggesting that there is more socioeconomic diversity in the body of individuals who have access to critical political information. As technology continues to improve, we hope that the costs of delivering online access to everyone will decrease. Over our period of study we have seen significant decreases in the digital divide and significant decreases in the divide over political use of the Internet as well. Being online together directly improves our sense of shared identity, particularly if we are sharing the same thing.

While we don't know to what extent this happens, we do know that people are at least exposed to enough similar information online that it updates their levels of political knowledge. That is, online access changes people's political knowledge. We see this within the small number of individuals whom we give free Internet and measure their political knowledge over 18 months (and compare this to a population that has had Internet access the entire time). People who have access to the Internet increase their base knowledge of standard political facts. Indeed, a literature has established that this proxy for political knowledge should predict an individual's ability to process complicated political campaigns and events, and furthermore allow strong democratic ideals such as the kinds of representation possible to be stable and supported. A politically informed public is a necessary component for a functioning participatory democracy. This feature is further supported by the increase in Google searches ahead of primary elections (seen from individual-level survey data) and the increase in Google searches in co-partisan general elections in California (seen from aggregate Google-Trends data). In individual-level survey data people report seeking out political information as well; over 58% of those who have Internet access report getting news about politics on the 2012 general election campaigns from online sources. Voters seek out political information online ahead of politically salient events. They are relying on online sources, and these online sources do indeed increase their political knowledge. Shared political knowledge also improves our sense of civic community, allows for meaningful engagement, and allows for more-informed citizens. The new media revolution has improved the way in which ordinary citizens can seek out political information.

When we focus on Twitter, we observe that not only are elites communicating directly to the voters but also they are making truthful statements about their partisan identities. To the extent to which we see deviations in this strategy, we note that these are places that are theoretically understood to have elected legislators with particularly strong homestyle, a form of trusted communication in which the district permits ideological deviance in exchange for deep trust and understanding. We observe this pattern in the rate of nonpartisan Twitter speech, but what this tells us is that the new media revolution is encouraging legislators to maintain the strategic communication profile that reflects not only the preferences of the district but also their actual legislative behavior. This provides voters with another channel to listen, it provides legislators with another channel to listen, and it provides researchers with the ability to monitor that conversation. The content of this conversation is encouraging for democracy. Receiving information from legislators, via new media, hasn't changed the strategic communication strategy of legislators much since our original notions about how legislators communicate with their districts, but what has changed is our ability to know what the content of that conversation is, and for voters to be able to engage with legislators directly more easily, through another channel.

The dark side of the new media revolution appears to be that the forums for public deliberation have simply not delivered what they promised. YouTube comments, online sharing, and posting of political content across social media seem rife with conflict as that communication often eliminates the fundamental fabric that connected individuals who were communicating offline, their personal ties and relationships help to buffer and mitigate political differences. Online political deliberation, while it occurs, appears to be absolutely worse than direct, personal conversation between friends, family, and neighbors.

Two main features of the new media revolution that we uncover—a reduction in the digital divide, and an expansion of political knowledge—are not the only encouraging findings. We have some suggestive evidence to support the idea that there is an association between becoming politically knowledgeable and becoming politically engaged. We see a strong association with Google searches for "vote" and actual turnout, for example. There are new ways of participating, such as the passive "likes" of political posts on the social media platform Facebook. To the extent to which these count as a form of signaling about social norms of politics, we see these opportunities as small ways to engage people who were otherwise politically unengaged, either because of restrictions on time, interest, or a willingness to tolerate political disagreement. These new opportunities allow a different kind of political deliberation. In our sample of survey respondents, over 21% who are online report they had taken the opportunity to comment about an online news story or blog post. Over 35% report they were solicited to participate actively in politics by email. There is a rising opportunity for ordinary citizens to be political opinion leaders. We refer to this as the rise of the sophisticates—there is an increased role for the "sharers" online. Over 18% of our survey respondents, when we are describing the typical American Internet voter, report they discuss politics online at least weekly. Yet, still the predominant way to talk about politics is via conversation with friends, family, and neighbors.

We also see several opportunities for improving the way that citizens engage with new media. While we observe some small amount of meaningful engagement in the YouTube comment forums, we also observe a general collapse of the norms of civility and conversation that stifles political deliberation. Regulation could police these interactions, with strategies such as moderating posts, punishing "trolls," or privileging civility with selective incentives.

BETTER CONSUMERS OF NEWS

Take a moment to pause and consider a breaking news story. What happened today, or yesterday, where you have seen an abundance of news coverage? You probably have an impression of what happened: the details of the event itself, the responsible parties, and how reliable the sources are that conveyed this information. In this pause, consider the following question: How do you know that your impression is accurate? How do you know if the news you followed was true? The digital revolution has made more information available to you than you ever imagined. It has been characterized by misinformation that news readers can access anytime, anywhere. The distinction between real journalism and citizen commentary, between pundits and professors, between propaganda and entertainment are more blurred now. It is harder, not easier, to determine the truth.

There is an inherent tension between viral and veritas. True stories are often more pedestrian than their fake alternatives, and appeals to conspiracy theories and in-group/out-group narratives may be hard-wired in our biology to be more interesting. It is a challenge to find and promote the truth. Yet, as new media matures, we increasingly see smarter solutions to the spread of outright fake stories or to the vitriolic hazing in public forums. We need to work on building more of these institutional solutions, and this is one way in which we can fight the spread of viral, fake media. Simply by moderating public forums or privileging civility online, "trolls," for example, can wind up with a quieter voice, while those individuals who want to engage in meaningful dialogue can have their voices amplified.

The other way we can move forward in terms of public consumption of media is in terms of norms. If individuals adopt norms of fact checking, then they are less likely to share fake stories. These norms include asking basic questions when consuming news such as those suggestions from the Newseum Media Literacy page: "Who made this? How was this made? Why was this made? When was this made? What is this missing? Where do I go from here?"[1] National Public Radio produced several recommendations on how listeners and readers can best consume breaking news. They write practical points, like, "Compare multiple sources" and "Don't trust stories that cite another news outlet as the source of the information." More insights include, "Read past headlines. Often they bear no resemblance to what lies beneath," and "Check the date. Social media often resurrects outdated stories." These are incredibly useful points for how each individual can better discern fact from fiction. There is a second part of their recommendation, though, which is particularly important to adopt. They say, "Beware reflexive retweeting. Some of this is on you."[2] Similarly, "Finally, if you're not sure it's true, don't share it! *Don't. Share. It.*"[3] Where the sharing of fake stories has the potential to spread most quickly and widely is in online social networks, such as Facebook. For example, you may have seen some of your friends on Facebook post, at one point or another, a statement such as "In response to the new Facebook guidelines, I hereby declare that my copyright is attached to all of my personal details, illustrations, comics, paintings, crafts, professional photos and videos, etc." This line about Facebook copyright is a fake story, and indeed one that has been covered extensively by reputable news sources such as the *New York Times*[4] and was publicly debunked by Snopes, a fact-checking website.[5] This viral story in fact raised such a ruckus that Facebook responded, stating "Anyone who uses Facebook owns and controls the content and information they post, as stated in our terms. They control how that content and information is shared. That is our policy, and it always has been." So why does this story continue to thrive? It seems to be a combination of the absence of a norm regarding fact-checking by users, and perhaps an underlying willingness to believe in conspiracy theories. If we could establish a social norm of sharing only verifiable media, the effects of fake media could be drastically reduced. While it is the case that the fake news creators are partially responsible, it is truly the responsibility of all of us to ensure that this information doesn't become a viral story. We regularly have social norms to preserve the integrity of our communities: we don't litter, even though of course just one person littering doesn't destroy a landscape. We recycle, even though just one household's worth of recycled goods doesn't preserve the environment. We vote, even though just one vote is unlikely to be pivotal. We should establish a similar norm about the sharing of fake news, because just one erroneous share has the capacity to affect multitudes of other people. Our ability to trust the political information we consume is not a luxury, but instead is critical to our democracy.

POLARIZATION AND THE INTERNET

Commentators often argue that Americans are becoming more polarized, that people on one end of the political or partisan spectrum do not communicate with or understand individuals on the other end of the spectrum. There is a large debate among political scientists as to whether the public is polarized or not. On the one hand, extensive data show that Americans are ideologically moderate, holding a mix of liberal and conservative positions. Even on issues that are seen as highly ideological, such as abortion, most people hold moderate, ambivalent positions (Fiorina et al. 2005; Fiorina and Abrams 2008; Glaeser and Ward 2006). These analyses suggest that ideological polarization is not a major issue in the United States.

However, even if the public is not ideologically polarized, there is evidence that Americans are becoming more polarized by political party. Abramowitz and Saunders (2004, 2005, 2008) have found that Americans are well-sorted by party and ideology: Democratic voters tend to be quite liberal while Republican voters tend to be quite conservative (Abramowitz and Saunders 2005). As people are becoming more sorted, they are becoming more politically active as well. Data from the American National Election Study (ANES) shows that more than one-quarter of all voters engaged in at least two political activities other than voting, and these people are very active in primary elections. There is also geographic polarization in the United States. States are more partisanly divided today than they were in the past, and counties are too. The fivethirtyeight blog reported that, in the 2016 election, 61% of voters voted in counties where either Trump or Clinton won 60% of the vote. Fewer than 10% of counties were decided by a margin of less than 10%. In 1992, only 39% of Americans lived in "landslide" counties.[6] Given that there is evidence that Americans are more polarized on partisan levels, what role has the Internet played in this polarization? Scholars at Brown University and Stanford

University have found that polarization rates are highest among older Americans, especially those over age 75, and are relatively low for people aged 18 to 39. Given what we know about age and Internet use, if the Internet was a key driver of polarization, then the findings of the research would be reversed.

As one of the authors noted, "Our findings don't rule out that the Internet has played some role in the recent rise in polarization. But they cast doubt on some common narratives linking polarization to online news and social media."[7] In their analysis, youth was the strongest predictor of using new media; 80% of people under age 30 use new media compared to fewer than 20% of the population over age 64. However, age was the strongest predictor of partisanship and polarization; those older than age 64 were much more partisan and polarized compared to the under-30 population.[8]

Scholars of radicalization also have found that it is offline activities and interactions, rather than online ones, that push people to become radicalized. Professors Peter Neumann and Shiraz Maher, of the International Centre for the Study of Radicalisation at King's College London recently wrote,

> Over the past five years, we have tracked the flow of foreign fighters into Syria and Iraq, collecting information on nearly 800 Western recruits—often including their social media footprints. Our experience and research suggests that radicalisation rarely happens exclusively online, and that the role of the internet is complex. The internet plays an important role in terms of disseminating information and building the brand of organisations such as IS, but it is rarely sufficient in replacing the potency and charm of a real-world recruiter.[9]

This analysis fits into the larger understanding of the role of face-to-face interactions in politics. When people talk face-to-face, it is a more effective way of interesting people in politics and political issues, especially if a person is not highly partisan or motivated already (Arceneaux and Nickerson 2009). Polarization and holding extreme views are not things that the Internet causes or that are unique to the Internet. Face-to-face discussions are far more likely to polarize people than is reading information through new media.

Reflection

The role that new media plays in our political system has changed and is changing the interaction between citizens, politicians, and media providers. Increasingly, citizens have more power. They have the power to seek out more information about politics. They have the power to become informed more easily, and to learn about government more quickly, than any generation that has come before them. What's more, the process of government is becoming increasingly transparent to them. Citizens can watch recordings of elected officials. A simple gaff can be recorded and repeated over and over, ensuring that elected officials are more careful and thoughtful in how they govern.

Yet, online sharing of information comes with yet another burden for participatory democracies. That is, citizens are not only responsible for their own information but also for their fellow citizens' information. They must avoid sharing fake political news. They have great forums for free speech, but they must own that speech, and they must take responsibility for the quality of that speech. To date, the results of the new media revolution are a little mixed. While citizens are better off in terms of acquiring political knowledge, we have yet to observe quality deliberation occur in online spaces. Online trolls have taken up residence in many of the places where there are possibilities for civic engagement. Will the next generation of citizens be responsible in setting up a new set of democratic norms?

We find the promise of the new media revolution has been met in terms of providing information and political knowledge. Citizens, and thus democracy, are better off because of the availability of political information online and the multiplicity of channels over which that information can be transmitted, particularly in those channels where representatives and candidates are able to communicate directly to voters. Yet, the new media revolution has failed to provide a meaningful community to generate civic engagement. This isn't impossible, but it hasn't happened yet.

OPPORTUNITIES FOR ENGAGEMENT AND FURTHER THOUGHT

Each chapter in this book has concluded with a section of further reading. At the close of the manuscript, we provide a number of avenues or strategies for students to engage with the new media revolution directly. The world desperately needs informed, civic-minded, thoughtful citizens and leaders. We challenge you to take the following list seriously and consider the ways in which active participation can improve both your understanding of government and also our democratic experiment itself.

1. Post a comment in an online political forum. Did your comment generate any responses? Do you feel the responses were based on quality information or a willingness to engage in deliberation? Or, do you feel like the quality of engagement is hostile to having real political conversation?
2. Now make the same comment, in person, to a friend, family member, or neighbor. What kind of a response did you have? How similar was it to the online conversation?
3. Impose a selective news blackout on the sources from which you typically get information. Consume news from a *new* specific channel—such as the *Wall Street Journal*—for 48 hours. Do not watch, read, or listen to the news during this time from your other sources, such as from Facebook, Twitter, or the *New York Times*. During this window, focus on the role these other sources played in forming your opinions.
4. Register to vote. Tweet, or write a Facebook post, on the page of an elected representative. Did you get a reply? Do the same thing via email. Did you get a reply? Now find a stamp and mail a letter. What happened?

5. Take a risk, and post information on your social media of choice about a political issue you care about. Using what you have learned in chapter 6, try to make it funny (and maybe include a kitten). Did anyone share it? Comment on it?

6. Take a moment to reflect on your own political choices. When you cast a ballot, do you make your choice based on what is in your own best interests, the best interests of your community, or the best interests if the country as a whole?

Notes

Preface

1. Gary King, Jennifer Pan, and Margaret E. Roberts, "How the Chinese Government Fabricates Social Media Posts for Strategic Distraction, not Engaged Argument," Working paper, 2016. http://j.mp/1Txxiz1.
2. S. F. Reardon and K. Bischoff, "The Continuing Increase in Income Segregation, 2007–2012," 2016, retrieved from Stanford Center for Education Policy Analysis: http://cepa.stanford.edu/content/continuing-increase-income-segregation-2007-2012.
3. Of course, the thoughtful among you likely realize that a world where there is both housing segregation and online polarization is a very narrow world indeed!
4. Katherine Cramer Walsh, *Talking about Politics: Informal Groups and Social Identity in American Life* (Chicago: University of Chicago Press, 2004).

Chapter 1

1. https://www.youtube.com/watch?v=MU9V6eOFO38
2. http://www.emc.com/collateral/analyst-reports/idc-the-digital-universe-in-2020.pdf
3. For example, see https://www.bostonglobe.com/news/nation/2013/08/10/brain-trust-for-sale-the-growing-footprint-washington-think-tank-industrial-complex/7ZifHfrLPlbz0bSeVOZHdI/story.html
4. https://www.crowdpac.com/about
5. Jim Crowe laws in the South were an example of groups engaging in factional politics to oppress a smaller group. In some cases, one group winning or losing is not generally problematic; if the "more bike lanes" groups win out over the "more basketball courts at parks" groups, it is the general trade-offs that are made in the political world. Factions are much more problematic when one group uses its power to affect another group's rights.
6. Again, remember this is also a time before remote controls; changing channels required actually getting up, turning the dial, and possibly then adjusting the antenna on the television until the picture was clear.
7. https://www.youtube.com/watch?v=r90z0PMnKwI. "Macaca" is the Portuguese word for monkey. It is a derogatory term that was used by colonial whites to refer to Africans.
8. See, for example, the attacks on Senator Bennett on www.redstate.com. http://www.redstate.

9. https://www.washingtonpost.com/politics/trump-recorded-having-extremely-lewd-conversation-about-women-in-2005/2016/10/07/3b9ce776-8cb4-11e6-bf8a-3d26847eeed4_story.html

10. http://www.slate.com/blogs/the_slatest/2016/10/09/trump_post_tape_polls_aren_t_as_devastating_as_they_could_be.html

11. https://www.vox.com/policy-and-politics/2016/11/1/13486968/clinton-ad-trump-sexual-assault-pussy-sexism

Chapter 2

1. https://www.youtube.com/watch?v=RwkNnMrsx7Q

2. For example, one of us posted a photo of the worn-out basketball nets at a public park on the Facebook page of the mayor, and, Voila!, new basketball nets were put up the following week.

3. http://www.coloradoindependent.com/147009/senate-moves-college-affordability-bill-house-works-to-better-serve-juvenile-offenders

4. When we say something "blows up" Twitter, it means that the topic is discussed by an enormous number of Twitter users.

5. Specifically, we ran a simple logit regression, where the dependent variable was "not using the Internet, even occasionally." The independent variables in the model were age, education, income, and race, using the categories that were discussed in the text. We used Clarify (King et al. 2000) to produce predicted probabilities that allow us to show how a change in each variable would affect the likelihood of not being online, compared to our baseline respondent.

6. http://pewInternet.org/Commentary/2012/February/Pew-Internet-Mobile.aspx

7. http://www.ctia.org/advocacy/research/index.cfm/aid/10323

8. http://www.pewhispanic.org/2012/02/21/statistical-portrait-of-hispanics-in-the-united-states-2010/#9

9. The differences between online and offline activities are statistically significant. To test this we performed a paired sample t-test, which allowed us to determine whether the difference in use of the online and offline activities were statistically significant. This statistic compares activities for online people only, since they were the ones who were asked both questions.

10. More details of the survey can be found here: http://taps.wustl.edu.

11. While this difference is not statistically significant (the p value for this test is .2), given the small numbers of observations available for this test, we view this result as highly suggestive.

12. http://www.politico.com/story/2016/01/sanders-fundraising-final-quarter-2015-217288

13. https://www.democracynow.org/2015/12/15/headlines/report_top_news_shows_give_trump_234_minutes_sanders_10_minutes

14. http://www.pewinternet.org/2017/05/17/tech-adoption-climbs-among-older-adults/

Chapter 3

1. One key difference between the NFL shows and the Sunday politics shows is that people under the age of 60 watch the NFL shows. The dominant demographic for Sunday political shows are older people.

2. An excellent explanation of the false consensus effect can be found in Lee Ross, David Greene, and Pamela House, "The False Consensus Effect: An Egocentric Bias in Social

Perception and Attribution Processes," *Journal of Experimental Social Psychology* 13, no. 3 (1977): 279–301.

3. If you find yourself following the presidential primary elections in the 11 months prior to the election year, it is likely a highly inefficient activity. For proof, just look at the polls and media coverage for Republicans in 2011, as candidates vied to be selected to run against President Barack Obama.

    If you started following the Republican primaries in 2011, you would probably have known a bit about Governor Mitt Romney or Representative Ron Paul; both had run for president in 2008. But the rest of the players you would have had to read up on. You would have known about Governor Tim Pawlenty (MN) and Congressman Thaddeus McCotter (MI), both of whom dropped out of the race after the Iowa straw poll in August. You would have read up on Congresswoman Michele Bachmann (MN), whose campaign ended in the very first contest (the Iowa Caucus on January 3, 2012), and Herman Cain, who suspended his campaign in December. You might have read that Governor Jon Huntsman Jr. was thoughtful and that Governor Rick Perry (TX) was a poor debater; both dropped out after the second primary election (the New Hampshire primary). Knowing these facts might have made you feel smarter, but, unless you lived in Iowa or New Hampshire, knowing about these candidates was not very helpful. It is much like following the NFL combines that occur before the NFL draft, and then being the person who knows who is up or down during the NFL preseason.

    Only four candidates were actively campaigning after the New Hampshire primary: Representative Newt Gingrich (GA), Representative Paul, Governor Romney, and Senator Rick Santorum (PA). To go back to the football analogy, these were the candidates who were competing in the regular season and the playoffs to determine who went to the Super Bowl—the general election.

4. Washington, Louisiana, and California all use a form of "Jungle Primary" for primary elections. In this type of primary, all candidates from both parties are on the ballot and the top two finishers compete in a general election (Washington and California) unless one candidate gets over 50% of the vote (Louisiana). Also, many local government primary elections are nonpartisan, where there are no party cues related to voting.

5. See, for example, Bimber (2003), Bimber and Davis (2003), Cornfield (2004), Frantsich (2002), and Graff (2007).

6. Anderson and Cornfield (2003), Bimber (2003), Cornfield (2004).

7. Mossberger et al. (2008), Best and Krueger (2005), Kenski and Stroud (2006), Drew and Weaver (2006), Dalrymple and Scheufele (2007), Hall and Sinclair (2011).

8. See, for example, Almond and Verba (1963), Berelson et al. (1954), Campbell et al. (1960), and Converse (1964).

9. See, for example, Mossberger et al. (2008), Best and Krueger (2005), and Kenski and Stroud (2006).

10. See, for example, Delli et al. (1996), Gilens et al. (2007), and Prior (2005).

11. See Graber (1984), Popkin (1994), Lupia (2006), Lupia and McCubbins (1998), Gibson and Caldeira (2009), and Boudreau (2009) for examples work in this area.

12. Go to http://electionstudies.org/studypages/anes_timeseries_2012/anes2012TS_codebook. pdf and search the pdf for "political knowledge" and you can see this. For the items listed here, all partial interviews and cases where the respondent was not asked the question are deleted. The percentages reflect these items being deleted.

13. See, for example, Boudreau (2009), Gibson and Caldeira (2009), Lupia (2006), Lupia and McCubbins (1998), and Prior and Lupia (2008).

14. Norrander (1996), Marshall (1983), Abramowitz (1989).
15. Lupia and McCubbins (1998).
16. For example, see Campbell (1983), Geer (1989), Marshall (1981, 1984), Norrander (1986b), Pfau et al. (1993, 1995), Stone et al. (1992), and Williams et al. (1976).
17. http://www.cc.com/video-clips/tyrqv8/the-nightly-show-the-state-of-obama
18. In the past, being a veteran was not a characteristic that was helpful in choosing a candidate; prior to President Clinton, all presidents since Franklin D. Roosevelt had a history of military service, at some level. Even FDR served as assistant secretary of the navy. Today, few politicians have served in the military—only 19% of members of Congress have any military experience. In the 1970s, upward of 70% of senators and a large percentage of House members had such experience.
19. Specifically, we pair state-level panel data of Google searches with three waves of individual-level panel data from the Cooperative Campaign Analysis Project (CCAP) conducted between January 2008 and November 2008. These data allow us to identify associations between the timing of primary elections and the search for online political information about the presidential primary candidates. We rely on variation in the scheduling of primary elections to understand the relationship between an individual's need for political information and the role of the Internet in politics.
20. Google reflects search data conducted using only one search engine and limits our analysis only to those who have Internet access. However, we have good reason to think that the behavior observed on Google is typical. By 2007, over 70% of Americans had access to the Internet and more than half of all searches in 2007 were performed on Google. Most importantly, Google users' characteristics are socioeconomically and demographically diverse and correlate with the characteristics of state residents (Stephens-Davidowitz 2013; Stephens-Davidowitz and Hal Varian 2014; Manzano and Ura 2013). Google Trends data are increasingly used by political scientists to study public opinion and politics. In this project, we use Google Trends data to look for aggregate evidence of political queries.
21. https://www.nytimes.com/2013/12/08/opinion/sunday/how-many-american-men-are-gay.html
22. https://www.nytimes.com/2015/12/13/opinion/sunday/the-rise-of-hate-search.html
23. https://campaignstops.blogs.nytimes.com/2012/06/09/how-racist-are-we-ask-google/
24. See https://techcrunch.com/2016/03/01/the-ap-debuts-election-buzz-a-tool-that-uses-twitter-and-google-data-to-track-the-u-s-elections/
25. This means that we exclude states where party primaries were held separately: Hawaii, Idaho, Kansas, Maine, Montana, Nebraska, New Mexico, Nevada, South Carolina, and Wyoming.
26. When we test this question statistically, we find that, ahead of each state's primary election, there are approximately .44 more normalized Google searches for Obama, McCain, Romney, or Clinton, on average. We estimate coefficients from a linear regression where the Google search volume serves as the dependent variable and the date of the primary election is the independent variable of interest. We code all dates ahead of the primary and the day of the primary as one, and all days after the primary as zero. A positive value for the pre-primary coefficient means that there is additional searching happening in advance of a state's primary. We include state fixed effects, recognizing the very real differences in campaign strategies employed by campaigns across the states that will affect both the supply of and demand for political information.
27. The CCAP was a six-wave panel survey with roughly 20,000 individual respondents completing all six waves. Survey waves were implemented in December 2007, and

January, March, August, October, and November (post-election) 2008. Core sets of questions were asked of all respondents and various research teams added individual content.

28. Because of the design of the CCAP, there are large numbers of survey respondents from each state, and so we have significant numbers of respondents in each of the three windows: 10.6% of respondents had the opportunity to participate in the first primary window (1,823), 71.4% were classified into the second primary window (12,233), and 18.0% were classified into the third primary window (3,082).

29. A respondent is "treated" if the respondent is in a pre-primary phase that is, has not yet had the opportunity to participate in a primary. We generate an indicator variable for whether the individual has yet to experience a primary election that takes on a value of 1 if an individual lives in a state where the primary election has not yet taken place, 0 otherwise. This allows an individual whose primary occurs after the second survey wave, for example, to be classified as pre-primary in both the first and second survey.

30. To test for the robustness of this estimate, we ran two models. The first is the simple model stated previously. The second model includes a number of control variables, including a measure of the respondent's political sophistication, race (black), gender (female), whether or not they are associated with a branch of the military, whether or not they consider themselves Mormon, and a seven-point party identification variable. Summary statistics for the variables in Figure 2.4 are presented in Table 2.3.

31. http://www.washingtonpost.com/wp-dyn/content/article/2008/02/18/AR20080 21802364.html

32. They control for the margin of victory of each legislator (to control for the competitiveness of the election), whether each legislator serves in a leadership position, and the previous amount of Google searching that occurred during an earlier search window in the previous election (to account for legislators who already had high public visibility).

33. The voter turnout data derives from the US Election Project, maintained by Professor Michael P McDonald, at http://www.electproject.org/home/voter-turnout. We exclude all states that report 0 searches, as this value is indistinguishable between missing data and the absence of any searching whatsoever. This gives us 142 observations, where the rate of searching and turnout have a positive linear relationship (linear regression coefficient of .152, standard error .058).

34. http://www.usatoday.com/story/news/politics/onpolitics/2016/01/26/google-tests-new-search-result-content-generated-campaigns/79329344/?utm_source=hs_email&utm_medium=email&utm_content=25731712&_hsenc=p2ANqtz-_qzLE1T9KIktBr8 hhxfjzHey15bTFich2Y9qopmCFJ1dtQTVGVP2V0BE3xvlRo06AyQw0iDz3X HejK8ftoL8tewd9wg&_hsmi=25731712

35. http://fortune.com/2016/03/02/trump-win-canada-searches/; and http://www.vox.com/ 2016/3/2/11146024/move-to-canada-super-Tuesday

36. http://searchengineland.com/ap-partners-with-google-twitter-to-follow-election-trends-243668

Chapter 4

1. https://www.washingtonpost.com/news/the-switch/wp/2016/03/25/inside-youtubes-explosive-transformation-of-american-politics/

2. As of April 7, 2016.

3. There are two ways that campaigns can reach viewers on YouTube. First are the actual videos posted by campaigns, such as the one described by the *Post*. The second is via advertisements. Before a YouTube video plays, it frequently opens with a 10- to 15-second

commercial. These commercials reach a vast audience that is frequently disconnected from traditional media. Because the YouTube audience is distinct and vast, political campaigns are incredibly interested in reaching viewers through this channel. In the early caucus and primary states of Iowa, New Hampshire, South Carolina, and Nevada, YouTube's open pool of reserved ad time sold out. In January, three political ads ranked among YouTube's 10 most-watched ads. Campaigns are producing free content for YouTube, and they are additionally purchasing ad time.

4. http://www.nytimes.com/2007/01/20/us/politics/20cnd-clinton.html
5. http://www.buzzfeed.com/jwherrman/who-has-the-worst-commenters-on-the-internet-an-i#.owvqGa3ee
6. http://www.motherjones.com/politics/2011/03/denial-science-chris-mooney
7. http://usuncut.com/politics/bernie-sanders-is-dominating-social-media/
8. https://www.washingtonpost.com/news/the-switch/wp/2016/03/25/inside-
9. http://www.timesofisrael.com/rnc-shuts-down-convention-live-chat-over-anti-semitic-rants/
10. http://www.nytimes.com/2007/01/20/us/politics/20cnd-clinton.html

Chapter 5

1. A Twitter user can tag a person in a tweet by using @ and then the Twitter name of the person they wish to see the message in their feed. For example, if Betsy (Betsysinclair1) sent a tweet saying "Seeing @hallthad in Chicago in 2 weeks!" this message would appear on Thad's Twitter feed.
2. This according to Twitters Official Twitter Account, December 18, 2012, https://twitter.com/ twitter/status/281051652235087872; and the Pew Research Centers Internet and American Life Project, August 2013, http://www.pewinternet.org/2013/08/05/72-of-online-adults-are-social-networking-site-users/.
3. http://www.businessinsider.com/twitter-has-a-surprisingly-small-number-of-us-users-2013-10 (April 30, 2014).
4. http://www.slate.com/articles/technology/technology/2014/05/twitter_is_not_dying_it_s_on_the_cusp_of_getting_much_bigger.html (May 1, 2014).
5. http://www.slate.com/articles/technology/technology/2014/05/twitter_is_not_dying_it_s_on_the_cusp_of_getting_much_bigger.html (May 1, 2014).
6. http://www.slate.com/articles/technology/technology/2014/05/twitter_is_not_dying_it_s_on_the_cusp_of_getting_much_bigger.html (May 1, 2014).
7. https://www.theatlantic.com/politics/archive/2013/04/youre-not-following-barackobama-twitter/316523/
8. http://www.thedailybeast.com/white-house-staff-congress-blindsided-by-fbi-pick-announcement?source=twitter&via=desktop
9. http://www.latimes.com/politics/washington/la-na-essential-washington-updates-donald-trump-names-fbi-director-pick-1496836465-htmlstory.html
10. https://www.thestreet.com/story/13896916/1/donald-trump-rode-5-billion-in-free-media-to-the-white-house.html
11. http://www.newyorker.com/tech/elements/the-rise-of-twitter-bots
12. http://www.gq.com/story/joe-mande-one-million-twitter-followers
13. https://www.fastcodesign.com/3031675/what-buying-twitter-bots-will-do-for-your-following
14. http://www.bbc.com/news/technology-37684418

15. http://www.newsweek.com/donald-trump-twitter-followers-fake-617873
16. https://www.bloomberg.com/news/articles/2016-11-17/trump-s-twitter-bots-turned-out-on-election-day
17. http://www.thedailybeast.com/how-pro-trump-twitter-bots-spread-fake-news
18. https://www.vox.com/world/2017/5/19/15561842/trump-russia-louise-mensch
19. https://www.oii.ox.ac.uk/blog/junk-news-and-bots-during-the-u-s-election-what-were-michigan-voters-sharing-over-twitter/
20. http://www.cbsnews.com/news/russian-bots-still-interfering-in-u-s-politics-after-election-expert/ and http://www.npr.org/sections/alltechconsidered/2017/04/03/522503844/how-russian-twitter-bots-pumped-outfake-news-during-the-2016-election
21. https://www.nytimes.com/2016/11/20/business/media/how-fake-news-spreads.html
22. https://www.psychologytoday.com/blog/contemporary-psychoanalysis-in-action/201612/fake-news-why-we-fall-it; http://news.nationalgeographic.com/2017/03/fake-news-science-psychology-quiz/; https://www.psychologytoday.com/blog/the-big-questions/201703/why-we-often-believe-fake-news; https://www.dartmouth.edu/~nyhan/nyhan-reifler.pdf

Chapter 6

1. https://www.statista.com/statistics/187041/us-user-age-distribution-on-facebook/
2. https://zephoria.com/top-15-valuable-facebook-statistics/
3. https://www.statista.com/statistics/187041/us-user-age-distribution-on-facebook/
4. Jessica Vitak, Paul Zube, Andrew Smock, Caleb T. Carr, Nicole Ellison, and Cliff Lampe, "It's Complicated: Facebook Users' Political Participation in the 2008 Election," *Cyber-Psychology, Behavior, and Social Networking* 14, no. 3 (2011): 107–114; Sebastien Valen-zuela, Namsu Park, and Kerk F. Kee, "Is There Social Capital in a Social Network Site? Facebook Use and College Students' Life Satisfaction, Trust, and Participation," *Journal of Computer Mediated Communication* 14, no. 4 (2009): 875–901; Sara Vissers and Dietlind Stolle, "Spill-Over Effects Between Facebook and On/Offline Political Participation? Evidence from a Two-Wave Panel Study," *Journal of Information Technology and Politics* 11, no. 3 (2014): 259–275.
5. Robert M. Bond, Christopher J. Fariss, Jason J. Jones, Adam D. I. Kramer, Cameron Marlow, Jaime E. Settle, and James H. Fowler, "A 61-Million-Person Experiment in Social Influence and Political Mobilization," *Nature* 489, no. 7415 (2012): 295–298.
6. The authors used verified voting data, where individuals from the study were matched against voting records to determine whether they had in fact voted.
7. https://www.theguardian.com/technology/2014/jun/29/facebook-users-emotions-news-feeds
8. This survey is called the Cooperative Congressional Election Study.
9. https://tinyurl.com/yakdmpc9
10. Nationally, the high levels of overreporting of turnout by individuals in the American National Election Survey (about 20%) suggests that many people subscribe to a social norm of voting and the high rates of false reporting appears to stem in large part from social pressure to vote (Karp and Brockington 2005; Silver et al. 1986).
11. https://www.buzzfeed.com/craigsilverman/top-fake-news-of-2016?utm_term=.mk2a08Ea3#.eh9va47vr
12. https://www.buzzfeed.com/craigsilverman/viral-fake-election-news-outperformed-real-news-on-facebook

13. https://www.buzzfeed.com/craigsilverman/top-fake-news-of-2016?utm_term=
.mk2a08Ea3#.eh9va47vr
14. https://web.stanford.edu/~gentzkow/research/fakenews.pdf
15. https://papers.ssrn.com/sol3/Delivery.cfm/SSRN_ID2960956_code2434952.pdf?
abstractid=2958246&mirid=1
16. For a reference, please see https://sheg.stanford.edu/.
17. https://www.cjr.org/tow_center/facebook_drains_fake_news_swamp_new_
experimental_partnerships.php
18. http://www.nytimes.com/2016/11/20/opinion/sunday/facebook-and-the-digital-
virus-called-fake-news.html?_r=0

Chapter 7

1. https://newseumed.org/activity/believe-it-or-not-putting-the-consumers-questions-
to-work/
2. http://www.wnyc.org/story/breaking-news-consumers-handbook-pdf/
3. http://www.wnyc.org/story/breaking-news-consumer-handbook-fake-news-edition
4. https://pogue.blogs.nytimes.com/2012/11/26/you-can-stop-spreading-that-face
book-notice-now/; https://www.nytimes.com/2015/09/29/technology/facebook-copyright-
hoax.html
5. http://www.snopes.com/computer/facebook/privacy.asp
6. https://fivethirtyeight.com/features/purple-america-has-all-but-disappeared/
7. https://phys.org/news/2017-03-political-polarization-dont-blame-web.html
8. https://www.brown.edu/Research/Shapiro/pdfs/age-polars.pdf

Bibliography

Abrajano, Marisa. 2015. "Reexamining the 'Racial Gap' in Political Knowledge." *Journal of Politics* 77(1): 44–54.

Abramowitz, Alan I. 1989. "Viability, Electability, and Candidate Choice in a Presidential Primary Election: A test of Competing Models." *The Journal of Politics.* 51,4: 977–992.

Abramowitz, Alan I. 2012. *The Polarized Public: Why American Government Is So Dysfunctional.* Pearson.

Abramowitz, Alan I., and Kyle L. Saunders. "Is polarization a myth?." *The Journal of Politics* 70.2 (2008): 542–555.

Abramowitz, Alan, and Kyle Saunders. "Why can't we all just get along? The reality of a polarized America." *The Forum.* Vol. 3. No. 2. De Gruyter, 2005.

Abramson, Paul R., John H. Aldrich, Phil Paolino, and David W. Rohde. 1992. "Sophisticated" Voting in the 1988 Presidential Primaries. American Political Science Review. 86(1): 55–69.

Adamic, L. 2005. "The Political Blogosphere and the 2004 U.S. Election: Divided They Blog." *BlogPulse, Intelliseek.* https://dl.acm.org/citation.cfm?id=1134277.

Alvarez, R. M., I. Levin, P. Mair, and A. Trechsel. 2014. "Party Preferences in the Digital Age." *Party Politics* 20(2): 227–236.

Alvarez, R. M., I. Levin, and J. A. Sinclair. 2012. "Making Voting Easier: Convenience Voting in the 2008 Presidential Election." *Political Research Quarterly* 65(2): 248–262.

Alvarez, R. M., I. Levin, A. H. Trechsel, and K. Vassil. 2014. "Voting Advice Applications: How Useful and for Whom?" *Journal of Information Technology and Politics* 11(1): 82–101.

Anderson, Ashley A., Dominique Brossard, Dietram A. Scheufele, Michael A. Xenos, and Peter Ladwig. "The "nasty effect:" Online incivility and risk perceptions of emerging technologies." *Journal of Computer-Mediated Communication*19, no. 3 (2014): 373–387.

Anderson, David M., and Michael Cornfield, eds. 2003. The Civic Web: Online Politics and Democratic Values. Rowman & Littlefield.

Arceneaux, Kevin, and David W. Nickerson. "Who is mobilized to vote? A re-analysis of 11 field experiments." *American Journal of Political Science* 53.1 (2009): 1–16.

Barabas, Jason, Jennifer Jerit, William Pollock, and Carlisle Rainey. 2014. "The Question(s) of Political Knowledge." *American Political Science Review* 108(4): 840–854.

Barbera, Pablo. 2015. "Birds of the Same Feather Tweet Together: Bayesian Ideal Point Estimation Using Twitter Data." *Political Analysis* 23(1): 76–91.

Barbera, Pablo, J. T. Jost, J. Nagler, J. A. Tucker, and R. Bonneau. 2015. "Tweeting from Left to Right: Is Online Political Communication More Than an Echo Chamber?" *Psychological Science*. 26(10):1531–1542.

Belli, Robert F., Michael W. Traugott, Margaret Young, and Katherine A. McGonagle. 1999. "Reducing Vote Over-Reporting in Surveys: Social Desirability, Memory Failure, and Source Monitoring." *Public Opinion Quarterly* 63: 90–108.

Berelson, Bernard R., Paul F. Lazarsfeld, William N. McPhee, and William N. McPhee. 1954. Voting: A Study of Opinion Formation in a Presidential Campaign. University of Chicago Press.

Best, Samuel J., and Brian S. Krueger. 2005. "Analyzing the Representativeness of Internet Political Participation." Political Behavior. 27,2: 183–216.

Bimber, Bruce. 2001. "Information and Political Engagement in America: The Search for Effects of Information Technology at the Individual Level." *Political Research Quarterly* 54: 53–67.

Bimber, Bruce. 2003. *Information and American Democracy*. Cambridge University Press.

Bimber, Bruce, and Richard Davis. 2003. *Campaigning Online*. Oxford University Press.

Bond, Robert M., Christopher J. Fariss, Jason J. Jones, Adam D. I. Kramer, Cameron Marlow, Jamie E. Settle, and James H. Fowler. 2012. "A 61-Million-Person Experiment in Social Influence and Political Mobilization." *Nature* 489: 295–298.

Boudreau, Cheryl. 2009. "Closing the Gap: When Do Cues Eliminate Differences Between Sophisticated and Unsophisticated Citizens?" *Journal of Politics* 71(3): 964–976.

Brady, Henry E., Sidney Verba, and Kay Lehman Schlozman. 1995. "Beyond SES: A Resource Model of Political Participation." *American Political Science Review* 89(2): 271–294.

Broncheck, M. S. 1997. *From Broadcast to Netcast: The Internet and the Flow of Political Information*. Harvard University Press.

Broockman, David E., and Timothy J. Ryan. 2015. "Preaching to the Choir: Americans Prefer Communicating to Copartisan Elected Officials." *American Journal of Political Science*. 60(4): 1093–1107.

Calfano, Brian Robert, and Aaron Kruse. 2016. "Beyond Surveillance: The Effects of Issue Ad Vividness and Anxiety on Information Use." *American Politics Research* 44(3): 1098–1122.

Cappella, Joseph N., and Kathleen Hall Jamieson. *Spiral of cynicism: The press and the public good*. Oxford University Press on Demand, 1997.

Campbell, Angus, Philip E. Converse, Warren E. Miller, and E. Donald. 1960. The American Voter.

Campbell, Angus. 1964. "Voters and Elections: Past and Present." The Journal of Politics. 26,4: 745–757.

Carpini, MX Delli. 2004. "Mediating Democratic Engagement: The Impact of Communications on Citizens' Involvement in Political and Civic Life." Handbook Of Political Communication Research. 357–394.

Christakis, Nicholas A., and James H. Fowler. 2009. *Connected: The Surprising Power of Our Social Networks and How They Shape Our Lives*. Little, Brown and Company.

Clausen, Aage. 1968. "Response Validity: Vote Report." *Public Opinion Quarterly* 32: 588–606.

Cohen, J. L. 2003. "Party over Policy: The Dominating Impact of Group Influence on Political Beliefs." *Journal of Personality and Social Psychology* 85: 808–822.

Cohen, Marty, David Karol, Hans Noel, and John Zaller. 2009. "The Party Decides: Presidential Nominations Before and After Reform." University of Chicago Press.

Cornfield, Michael. 2004. Politics Moves Online: Campaigning and the Internet. The Century Foundation.

Dahl, Robert A. 1989. *Democracy and Its Critics*. Yale University Press.

Dalrymple, Kajsa E., and Dietram A. Scheufele. 2007. "Finally Informing the Electorate? How the Internet Got People Thinking about Presidential Politics in 2004." *Harvard International Journal of Press/Politics* 12,3: 96–111. DeBell, Matthew. 2013. "Harder Than It Looks: Coding Political Knowledge on the ANES." *Political Analysis* 21(4): 393–406.

Delli Carpini, Michael X., and Bruce A. Williams. 1996. "Constructing Public Opinion: The Uses of Fictional and Nonfictional Television in Conversations about the Environment." *The Psychology of Political Communication*.

Dixon, Julie. 2011. "Slacktivists Doing More Than Clicking in Support of Causes." http://static.scs.georgetown.edu/upload/kb_file/csic/OPR_SM_ GT_Slacktivists_ FINAL.pdf.

Drew, Dan, and David Weaver. 2006. "Voter Learning in the 2004 Presidential Election: Did the Media Matter?" Journalism & Mass Communication Quarterly 83,1: 25–42.

Esterling, Kevin M., David M. J. Lazer, and Michael A. Neblo. 2011. "Representative Communication: Web Site Interactivity and Distributional Path Dependence in the US Congress." *Political Communication* 28(4): 409–439.

Etzioni, Amitai. 1993. *The Spirit of Community: Rights, Responsibilities and the Communitarian Agenda*. Crown Publishers.

Fenno, Richard F. *The challenge of congressional representation*. Harvard University Press, 2013.

Fenno, Richard F. 1978. *Home Style: House Members in Their Districts*. Longman Classics.

Fiorina, Morris P., and Samuel J. Abrams. 2008. "Political Polarization in the American Public." *Annual Review of Political Science* 11: 563–588.

Fiorina, Morris P., Samuel J. Abrams, and Jeremy C. Pope. 2005. *Culture War? The Myth of a Polarized America*. Pearson Longman.

Frantzich, Stephen E. 2002. Cyberage Politics 101: Mobility, Technology, and Democracy. P. Lang Publishing Co. Frantzich, Stephen E. 2002. *Cyberage Politics 101: Mobility, Technology, and Democracy*. P. Lang Publishing Co.

Funk, Carolyn L. 2001. "Process Performance: Public Reaction to Legislative Policy Debate." In What Is It About Government That Americans Dislike? ed. John R. Hibbing and Elizabeth TheissMorse. New York: Cambridge University Press

Geer, John Gray. 1989. *Nominating Presidents: An Evaluation of Voters and Primaries*. No. 236. Greenwood Publishing Group.

Gentzkow, Matthew, and Jesse Shapiro. 2011. "Ideological Segregation Online and Offline." *Quarterly Journal of Economics* 126: 1799–1839.

Gentzkow, Matthew, Jesse M. Shapiro, and Matt Taddy. 2016. "Measuring Polarization in High-Dimensional Data: Method and Application to Congressional Speech." Working paper.

Gibson, James L., and Gregory A. Caldeira. 2009. "Knowing the Supreme Court? A Reconsideration of Public Ignorance of the High Court." *Journal of Politics* 71(2): 429–441.

Gilens, Martin. 2001. "Political Ignorance and Collective Policy Preferences." *American Political Science Review* 95(2): 379–396.

Gilens, Martin, Lynn Vavreck, and Martin Cohen. 2007. "The Mass Media and the Public's Assessments of Presidential Candidates, 1952-2000." *Journal of Politics*. 69,4: 1160–1175.

Glaeser, Edward L., and Bryce A. Ward. 2006. "Myths and Realities of American Political Geography." *Journal of Economic Perspectives* 20(2): 119–144.

Glassman, Matthew Eric, Jacob R. Strauss, and Colleen J. Shogan. 2011. "'Social Networking and Constituent Communications: Member Use of Twitter During a Two-Month Period in the 111th Congress.'" *Journal of Communications Research*.

Gottfried, Jeffrey, Michael Barthel, Elisa Shearer, and Amy Mitchell. 2016. "The 2016 presidential campaign–A news event that's hard to miss." *Pew Research Center.*

Graber, Doris. 1984. *Processing the News: How People Tame the Information Tide.* Longman.

Graber, Doris A., and Johanna Dunaway. 2015. *Mass Media and American Politics.* Sage.

Grimmer, Justin. 2013. *Representational Style in Congress: What Legislators Say and Why It Matters.* Cambridge University Press.

Habermas, Jürgen. 1989. The Structural Transformation of the Public Sphere. trans. Thomas Burger. Cambridge: MIT Press.

Habermas, Jürgen, Sara Lennox, and Frank Lennox. 1974. "The Public Sphere: An Encyclopedia Article (1964)." *New German Critique* 3: 49–55.

Haidt, Jonathan. "The moral emotions." *Handbook of affective sciences* 11.2003 (2003): 852–870.

Hall, Thad E., and Betsy Sinclair. 2011. "The American Internet Voter." *Journal of Political Marketing.* 10.1-2: 58–79.

Huckfeldt, Robert, and John Sprague. 1995. *Citizens, Politicism and Social Communication.* Cambridge University Press.

Jamieson, Kathleen Hall. 1997. *Civility in the House of Representatives: A background report.* Annenberg Public Policy Center.

Jennings, M. Kent, and Vicki Zeitner. 2003. "Internet Use and Civic Engagement." *Public Opinion Quarterly.* 67: 311–334.

Karp, Jeffrey A., and David Brockington. 2005. "Social Desirability and Response Validity: A Comparative Analysis of Overreporting Voter Turnout in Five Countries." *Journal of Politics* 67 (3): 825–840.

Kelly, J., D. Fisher, and M. Smith. 2005. "Debate, Division, and Diversity: Political Discourse Networks in USENET Newsgroups." Paper presented at the Stanford Online Deliberation Conference DIAC '05.

Kenski, Kate, and Natalie Jomini Stroud. 2006. "Connections between Internet Use and Political Efficacy, Knowledge, and Participation." Journal of Broadcasting & Electronic Media. 50,2: 173–192.

King, Gary, Michael Tomz, and Jason Wittenberg. 2000. "Making the Most of Statistical Analyses: Improving Interpretation and Presentation." *American Journal of Political Science* 44: 347–361.

Krebs, Valdis. 2004. "Working in the Connected World: Book Network." *IHRIM Journal.* 4(1): 87–90.

Lassen, David S., and Adam R. Brown. 2011. "Twitter the Electoral Connection?" *Social Science Computer Review* 29(4): 419–436.

Lawless, Jennifer. 2012. "Twitter and Facebook." In Richard L. Fox and Jennifer M. Ramos, eds., *iPolitics: Citizens, Elections, and Governing in the New Media Era.* Cambridge University Press. 206–232.

Lelkes, Yphtach, Gaurav Sood, and Shanto Iyengar. 2015. "The Hostile Audience: The Effect of Access to Broadband Internet." *American Journal of Political Science.*

Lupia, Arthur. 1994. "Shortcuts Versus Encyclopedias: Information and Voting Behavior in California Insurance Reform Elections." *American Political Science Review* 88(1): 63–76.

Lupia, Arthur. 2006. "How Elitism Undermines the Study of Voter Competence." *Critical Review* 18(1–3): 217–232.

Lupia, Arthur, and Mathew D. McCubbins. 1998. *The Democratic Dilemma: Can Citizens Learn What They Need to Know?* Cambridge University Press.

Manzano, Sylvia, and Joseph D. Ura. 2013. "Desperately Seeking Sonia? Latino Heterogeneity and Geographic Variation in Web Searches for Judge Sonia Sotomayor." *Political Communication.* 30,1: 81–99.

Marshall, Thomas R. 1983. "Evaluating Presidential Nominees: Opinion Polls, Issues, and Personalities." *Western Political Quarterly* 36,4: 650–659.

Marshall, Thomas R. 1981. *Presidential Nominations in a Reform Age.* Praeger Publishers.

McAdam, Doug. 1986. "Recruitment to High-Risk Activism: The Case of Freedom Summer." *American Journal of Sociology* 92(1): 64–90.

Mergel, Ines. 2012. "Connecting to Congress: The Use of Twitter by Members of Congress." *ZPB: The Journal for Political Consulting and Policy Advice* 5(3):108–114.

Miller, Joanne M., Kyle L. Saunders, and Christina E. Farhart. 2015. "Conspiracy Endorsement as Motivated Reasoning: The Moderating Roles of Political Knowledge and Trust." *American Journal of Political Science* 60(4): 824–844.

Mitchell, Amy, Jeffrey Gottfried, Jocelyn Kiley, and Katerina Eva Matsa. "Political polarization & media habits." *Pew Research Center* 21 (2014).

Mondak, Jeffrey J. 2001. "Developing Valid Knowledge Scales." *American Journal of Political Science* 45: 224–238.

Mossberger, Karen, Caroline J. Tolbert, and Ramona S. McNeal. 2007. Digital Citizenship: The Internet, Society, and Participation. MIT Press.

Mutz, D. C. 2002. "The Consequences of Cross-Cutting Networks for Political Participation." *American Journal of Political Science* 46(4): 838–855.

Mutz, D. C. 2008. "Is Deliberative Democracy a Falsifiable Theory?" *Annual Review of Political Science* 11: 521–538.

Mutz, Diana C., and Byron Reeves. 2005. "The new videomalaise: Effects of Televised Incivility on Political Trust." American Political Science Review 99(1): 1–15.

Negroponte, Nicholas. 1996. *Being Digital.* Vintage.

Nisbet, Matthew C. and Dietram A. Scheufele. 2007. The future of public engagement. *Scientist* **21**: 38–44.

Norrander, Barbara. 1986. "Correlates of Vote Choice in the 1980 Presidential Primaries." *The Journal of Politics.* 48,1: 156–166.

Norrander, Barbara. 1986. "Correlates of Vote Choice in the 1980 Presidential Primaries." The Journal of Politics 48(1): 156–166.

Norrander, Barbara. 1986. "Selective Participation: Presidential Primary Voters as a Subset of General Election Voters." *American Politics Quarterly* 14.1–2 (1986): 35–53.

Norrander, Barbara. 1996. "Presidential Nomination Politics in the Post-Reform Era." Political Research Quarterly 49(4): 875–915.

Norris, Pippa. 2001. *Digital Divide: Civic Engagement, Information Poverty and the Internet Worldwide.* Cambridge University Press.

Norris, Pippa. 2012. *Making Democratic Governance Work: The Impact of Regimes on Prosperity: Welfare and Peace.* Cambridge University Press.

Oliver, J. Eric, and Thomas J. Wood. 2014. "Conspiracy Theories and the Paranoid Style(s) of Mass Opinion." *American Journal of Political Science* 58(4): 952–966.

Papacharissi, Z. 2004. "Democracy Online: Civility, Politeness, and the Democratic Potential of Online Political Discussion Groups." *New Media and Society* 6(2): 259–283.

Pfau, Michael, Tracy Diedrich, Karla M. Larson, and Kim M. Van Winkle. 1993. "Relational and Competence Perceptions of Presidential Candidates During Primary Election Campaigns." *Journal of Broadcasting & Electronic Media.* 37,3: 275–292.

Pfau, Michael, Tracy Diedrich, Karla M. Larson, and Kim M. Van Winkle. 1995. "Influence of Communication Modalities on Voters' Perceptions of Candidates During Presidential Primary Campaigns." *Journal of Communication.* 45,1: 122–133.

Popkin, Samuel L. 1994. *The Reasoning Voter: Communication and Persuasion in Presidential Campaigns.* University of Chicago Press.

Prior, Markus. 2007. Post-Broadcast Democracy: How Media Choice Increases Inequality in Political Involvement and Polarizes Elections. Cambridge University Press.

Prior, Markus. 2005. "News vs. Entertainment: How Increasing Media Choice Widens Gaps in Political Knowledge and Turnout." *American Journal of Political Science* 49(3): 577–592.

Prior, Markus, and Arthur Lupia. 2008. "Money, Time, and Political Knowledge: Distinguishing Quick Recall and Political Learning Skills." *American Journal of Political Science.* 52,1: 169–183.

Putnam, Robert D. 2000. *Bowling Alone: The Collapse and Revival of American Community.* Simon and Schuster.

Radford, Jason, and Betsy Sinclair. "Electronic Homestyle: Tweeting Ideology." (2016). Manuscript: University of Chicago.

Rolfe, Meredith. 2012. Voter Turnout: A Social Theory of Political Participation. Cambridge University Press.

Schlozman, Kay Lehman, Sidney Verba, and Henry E. Brady. 2010. "Weapon of the Strong? Participatory Inequality and the Internet." *Perspectives on Politics* 8(2): 487–509.

Schlozman, Kay Lehman, Sidney Verba, and Henry E. Brady. 2013. *The Unheavenly Chorus.* Princeton University Press.

Sigelman, Lee, and David Bullock. "Candidates, issues, horse races, and hoopla: Presidential campaign coverage, 1888–1988." *American Politics Quarterly* 19.1 (1991): 5–32.

Silver, Brian D., Barbara A. Anderson, and Paul R. Abrahamson. 1986. "Who Overreports Voting?" *American Political Science Review* 80 (2): 613–624.

Sinclair, Betsy. 2012. *The Social Citizen*. University of Chicago Press.

Sinclair, Betsy, Margaret McConnell, and Donald P. Green. 2012. "Detecting Spillover in Social Networks: Design and Analysis of Multilevel Experiments." *American Journal of Political Science* 56(4): 1055–1069.

Sinclair, Betsy, Margaret McConnell, and Melissa R. Michelson. 2013. "Local Canvassing and Social Pressure: The Efficacy of Grassroots Voter Mobilization." *Political Communication* 30(1): 52–57.

Sinclair, Betsy, and Michael Wray. 2015. "Googling the Top Two: Information Search in California's Top Two Primary." *California Journal of Public Policy* 7(1): 1–12.

Smith, Marc A., Lee Rainie, Ben Shneiderman, and Itai Himelboim. "Mapping Twitter topic networks: From polarized crowds to community clusters." *Pew Research Center* 20 (2014).

Sniderman, Paul M., Richard A. Brody, and Philip E Tetlock. 1991. *Reasoning and Choice*. Cambridge University Press.

State, Bogdan, and Lada Adamic. 2015. "The Diffusion of Support in an Online Social Movement: Evidence from the Adoption of Equal-Sign Profile Pictures." In *Proceedings of the 18th ACM Conference on Computer Supported Cooperative Work and Social Computing*: 1741–1750.

Street, Alex, Thomas A. Murray, John Blitzer, and Rajan S. Patel. 2015. "Estimating Voter Registration Deadline Effects with Web Search Data." *Political Analysis. 23*(2): 225–241.

Stephens-Davidowitz, Seth, and Hal Varian. 2014. "A Hands-On Guide to Google Data." Tech. Rep.

Stephens-Davidowitz, Seth. "The Cost Of Racial Animus on a Black Presidential Candidate: Using Google Search Data to Find What Surveys Miss." (2013).

Stone, Walter J., Lonna Rae Atkeson, and Ronald B. Rapoport. 1992. "Turning On or Turning Off? Mobilization and Demobilization Effects of Participation in Presidential Nomination Campaigns." *American Journal of Political Science*. 665–691.

Suler, John. "The online disinhibition effect." *Cyberpsychology & behavior* 7.3 (2004): 321–326.

Sunstein, Cass R. 2001. *Republic.com*. Princeton University Press.

Sunstein, Cass R. 2007. *Republic.com 2.0*. Princeton University Press.

Thompson, Dennis F. 2008. Deliberative Democratic Theory and Empirical Political Science. Annual Review of Political Science. 11: 497–520.

Traugott, Michael W., and John P. Katosh. 1979. "Response Validity in Surveys of Voting Behavior." *Public Opinion Quarterly* 43: 359–577.

Trippi, Joe. 2008. *The Revolution Will Not Be Televised*. Harper.

Uslaner, Eric M. 1993. The Decline of Comity in Congress. Ann Arbor: University of Michigan Press.

Verba, Sidney, and Gabriel Almond. 1963. "The Civic Culture." Political Attitudes and Democracy in Five Nations.

Verba, Sidney, Kay Lehman Schlozman, and Henry E. Brady. 1995. *Voice and Equality.* Harvard University Press.

Vitak, J., P. Zube, A. Smock, C. T. Carr, N. Ellison, and C. Lampe. 2011. "It's Complicated: Facebook Users' Political Participation in the 2008 Election." *Cyberpsychology, Behavior and Social Networking* 14(3): 107–114.

Williams, D. C., Weber, S. J., Haaland, G. A., Mueller, R. H., & Craig, R. E. 1976. Voter Decisionmaking in a Primary Election: An Evaluation of Three Models of Choice. *American Journal of Political Science*, 37–49.

Yardi, Sarita, and Danah Boyd. 2010. "Dynamic Debates: An Analysis of Group Polarization over Time on Twitter." *Bulletin of Science Technology and Society* 30(5): 316–327.

Index

Page numbers followed by *f* and *t* refer to figures and tables, respectively.

ABC, 11
Abramowitz, A. I., 121
Abramson, P. R., 57
Access Hollywood, 14
accessibility, 16
accountability, 8, 122–23
active citizenship, 7–9, 53
age
    and Internet use, 23–26, 23*f*, 25*f*, 27*f*,
      32*f*–33*f*, 49
    and social networking site use, 36*f*
    and Twitter use, 35*f*
Allen, George, 14
American Internet voter, 48–51
American National Election Study
    (ANES), 26, 41–43, 56, 84, 121
American Panel Survey (TAPS), 28–29,
    45–46
Anderson, A. A., 77
ANES. *See* American National
    Election Study
anonymity, 78
authoritarian countries, xvi–xvii

Barack, Obama, 3
Barbera, Pablo, 80, 93–94
BBS (bulletin board systems), 34
Bennett, Bob, 14
bias, 99, 102–3
Biden, Joe, 58
big data, defined, 2
Bimber, Bruce, 31

bipartisan commenting community,
    85–86
blind spot, bias, 103
Bloggers, 30*t*
"blows up," defined, 126*n*4
Bond, Robert, 106
bots, on Twitter, 99–101
Brady, Henry, 10, 19, 98–99
bulletin board systems (BBS), 34
Bush, George W., 58, 68–69, 81*f*–83*f*
BuzzFeed, 75, 113

California, primaries in, 65–67, 127*n*4
campaigning, in primary elections, 63–64
candidate information, googling for,
    62–65
Carson, Ben, 81*f*–83*f*
CCAP (Cooperative Campaign Analysis
    Project), 62–65, 70
cell phones, 31–34, 33*f*
channel, on YouTube, 86
Chavez, Rocky, 66
citizenship, xv–xviii, 7–9, 53, 123–24. *See*
    also digital citizens
Citizens United v. FEC, xix
civil rights protests, 77
Clinton, Hillary
    and Bernie Sanders, 48
    googling of, 58, 64–65, 68
    and Twitter, 100–101
    and YouTube, 73, 81*f*–83*f*, 86–89
CNN, 11

Colorado Independent, 20
comments
    about presidential elections, 81*f*–83*f*
    frequency of, 81*f*
    importance of, 75
    on YouTube, 79–85
communication
    political, xiii, 39, 39*t*
    through Twitter, 93–96
    on YouTube, 87–89
communities
    bipartisan commenting, 85–86
    interactive user (*See* interactive
        user communities)
    social media, 29–30
confirmation bias, 102
conspiracy theories, xvii–xviii
Cooperative Campaign Analysis Project
    (CCAP), 62–65, 70, 128*n*27, 129*n*28
Cruz, Ted, 68, 81*f*–83*f*

"Daily Me," 11–12
Dean, Howard, 18–20, 47–48
decision-making, 4–9, 57, 78
deliberation, political. *See* political
    deliberation
Democracy Now, 48
democratic values, and googling, 69–72
de Tocqueville, Alexis, 7
digital citizens, 18–51
    American Internet voter, 48–51
    and Bernie Sanders, 47–48
    cell phones affecting, 31–34
    and Howard Dean, 18–20
    new media access by, 20–37
    offline adults, 22–28
    online access points for, 28–29
    political Americans, 37–44
    politically disinterested, 45–47
    social Internet adults, 34–37
    social media communities for, 29–30
discussion bubbles, on YouTube, 85–86
Dodd, Chris, 58

education
    and Internet use, 23–26, 23*f,* 25*f,* 27*f,*
        32–34, 32*f*–33*f*
    and social networking site use, 36*f*
    and Twitter use, 35*f*
Edwards, John, 18, 58

elections. *See* presidential elections;
        primary elections
email, 39*t,* 40
emotional language, on Facebook, 99, 107
Empowerment Age, The, 50
engagement, political. *See* political
        engagement

Facebook
    and fake news, 114
    impact of, 106–7, 116
    revolution of, in Egypt, 21–22
    use of, 29, 30*t*
face-to-face interactions, 122
fact checking, 120–21
fake news, 101–3, 113–15, 120–21
false consensus effect, 52
Federalist Papers, 7
fedspending.org, 14
Fenno, Richard, 96
football, 52–53, 126*n*2

gender
    and Internet use, 23–26, 23*f,* 25*f,* 27*f,*
        32*f*–33*f*
    and online searching, 64
    and social networking site use, 36*f*
    and Twitter use, 35*f*
Gentzkow, Matthew, 85–86, 104
Georgetown University, 84
Gerber, Alan, 106
Gingrich, Newt, 53, 127*n*3
Giuliani, Rudy, 58
good citizenship, xv–xviii, 123–24
Google, 128*n*20
Google plus, 30*t*
Google Trends, 60, 62, 66, 128*n*20
googling, 52–72
    for candidate information, 62–65
    and democratic values, 69–72
    importance of, 52–55
    for political knowledge, 55–56, 118
    during presidential elections, 67–69
    during primary elections, 56–61,
        65–67
    volume of, 67*f*
Gore, Al, 18
government, structure of, 4
GQ magazine, 100
Gravel, Mike, 58

Green, Donald, 106
Grimmer, Justin, 94

Habermas, J., 8
Hodges, Sherry, 66
Huckabee, Mike, 58

identity, shared, xvi, 4–5
implicit bias, 102
incivility, 76–79
income
   and Internet use, 23–26, 23f, 25f,
     32–34, 32f–33f, 49
   and social networking site use,
     36–37, 36f
   and Twitter use, 35f
information gap, 9–10
information sharing, 11–12, 31t
interactive user communities, xiii–xiv
   for digital citizens, 29–30
   as gated, xvii
   YouTube as (*See* YouTube)
   See also social media
Internet
   absence of, xviii–xix
   access to, 26, 27f, 32f–33f, 50, 118,
     129n20
   campaigning through, 18
   challenges to studies of, 117
   citizenship improving through, 8–9
   evolution of, 31
   impact of, 13
   polarization and, 121–23
   use of, 23–26, 23f, 25f, 38t, 117
   See also googling

Jim Crowe laws, 125n5
Jungle Primary, 127n4

Kasich, John, 68
Kelly, J., 78–79
Kerry, John, 18
knowledge, political. *See* political
   knowledge
Kucinich, Dennis, 58

Lewandowski, Corey, 91
Limbaugh, Rush, 102
Lingle, Linda, 88
Los Angeles Times, 97

Lotan, Gilad, 100
Lowry, Trump, 91

Maher, Shiraz, 122
Mande, Joe, 100
McAdam, Doug, 112
McCain, John, 15, 58
McConnell, Mitch, 15
memberships, with interactive user
   communities, xiii
memes, 105, 111–12, 111f–112f, 115
Miller, J. M., xviii
moral emotions, 98–99
Mother Jones, 1–3
Mubarak, Hosni, 21
Mutz, D. C., 77, 87
Myspace, 30t

naive realism, 102
"nasty effect," 77
National Public Radio, 120
National Review, 91
NBC, 11
Negroponte, N., 11–12
Neumann, Peter, 122
New Hampshire, primary results vs.
   searches in, 69f, 127n4
new media, 1–17
   absence of, xviii–xix
   access to, 20–37, 28–29
   defined, xiii–xiv
   digital sharing through, 1–3
   effects of, xiii–xv
   future directions for, 120
   and good citizenship, xv–xviii
   and missing political utopia, 9–14
   opportunities/challenges of, 16–17
   and political decision-making,
     4–9
   political participation through, 49
   problems with, xvii, 119
   and pussygate, 14–16
   sharing through, 110–11
news, source of, 28–29, 28t–29t, 38t,
    107–9, 108t. *See also* fake news
Newseum Media Literacy page, 120
Newsweek, 100
New Yorker, The, 99–100
New York Times, 60, 88, 101, 115
Nightly Show, The, 58

Norrander, B., 57
Norris, Pippa, 21

Obama, Barack
    googling of, 56, 58, 64–65
    memes of, 112, 112*f*
    and Twitter, 97
    and YouTube, 87
OFA (Organizing for Action), 97
offline adults, 22–28, 22*f*, 23*f*, 25*f*
OII (Oxford Internet Institute), 100–101
Oliver, J. E., xvii–xviii
on-demand access, xiii
online sharing, 105–16
    content of, 107–9
    on Facebook, 106–7
    and fake news, 113–14
    of memes, 111–12
    prevalence of, 110–13
    and sharers vs. talkers, 109–10
    through new media, 1–3
opensecrets.org, 14
Oremus, William, 92–93
Organizing for Action (OFA), 97
Oxford Internet Institute (OII),
    100–101

Papacharissi, Z., 76
participation, political. *See* political
    participation
participatory democracy, xv, xvi, 69
Paul, Ron, 53, 58, 127*n*3
pay-by-text technologies, 6
Pence, Mike, 15
perception, and YouTube, 76–79
Pew Internet and American Life Projects,
    22–23, 32, 34, 37, 41–43
Pew Research Center, 13, 50, 92, 115–16
polarization, and Internet, 121–23
political Americans, 37–44
political communications, xiii, 39, 39*t*
political decision-making, 4–9
political deliberation, 3, 74–76, 119
political engagement, 6–7, 19, 41, 42*f*
political facts, knowledge vs., 55–56
"political junkies," 52
political knowledge
    googling for, 55–56
    increase in, 119
    and Internet access, 46–47, 118

measuring, 54
    through new media, 5–6
politically disinterested digital citizens,
    45–47
political participation
    new media increasing, 12–13
    online, 40–41, 41*t*, 42*f*, 44*t*, 49
    through Facebook, 106
political party, 27, 27*f*, 43
political utopia, and new media, 9–14
Politico, 90
popularity, on Twitter, 99–100
president, use of Twitter, 97–99
presidential elections, 67–69, 67*f*–69*f*,
    81*f*–83*f*
Priebus, Reince, 15
primary elections, 53, 56–61, 61*t*,
    65–67, 127*n*4
Prior, Markus, 11, 77
Proposition 14 (California), 66
protests, civil rights, 77
pussygate, 14–16
Putnam, Robert, 88

race
    and Internet use, 23–26, 23*f*, 25*f*, 27*f*,
        32–34, 32*f*–33*f*, 117
    and online searching, 64
    and social networking site use, 36*f*, 37
    and Twitter use, 35*f*
racism, 98
Radford, J., 94–95
radicalization, 122
radio, 4–5
realism, naive, 102
recovery.gov, 14
Reeves, B., 77
regulations.com, 14
religion, 56, 65
representativeness heuristic, 21
Richardson, Bill, 58
Roberts, John, 55
Rolfe, Meredith, 10
Romney, Mitt
    googling of, 53, 56, 58, 127*n*3
    memes of, 112, 112*f*
    and transparency, 1–3, 14–15
    and YouTube, 1–2
Rubio, Marco, 68–69, 81*f*–83*f*
Russia, 101

Sanders, Bernie, 47–48, 68, 81*f*–83*f*
Santorum, Rick, 53
Saunders, K. L., 121
Schlozman, Kay Lehman, 10, 13, 19
Shapiro, Jesse, 85–86
shared identity, xvi, 4–5
sharers, talkers vs., 109–10, 119
sharing, information, 11–12, 31*t*
Sinclair, Betsey, 66, 94–95
slacktivism, 84, 110
Slate.com, 15
smartphones, 50. *See also* cell phones
Snelling, Richard A., 18
social Internet adults, 34–37
social media
    campaigning through, 19
    evolution of, 34
    use of, 30*t*, 31*t*
    and viral information, 2–3
    in younger generations, 13
social media communities, 29–30
social networking sites, 36, 36*f*, 38*t*
Spicer, Sean, 97
Stanford Center for Education Policy
    Analysis, xix
Stephens-Davidowitz, Seth, 12
strategic voting, 53
streaming news, 5
Street, A., 67
Suler, J., 78
Sunstein, Cass, 4, 11
Sysomos, 92

talkers, sharers vs., 109–10
TAPS (American Panel Survey), 28–29,
    45–46
targeting, 6–7
television, 4, 11
Thompson, Fred, 58
transparency, 2, 13–14, 87–88, 103
Trippi, John, 50
Trump, Donald
    googling of, 68, 71
    and pussygate, 14–16
    speeches on YouTube, 86–87
    and Twitter, 90–91, 97–99,
        100–101
    and YouTube, 74, 81*f*–83*f*
trust, 13
Tumblr, 30*t*

Twitter, 90–104, 118–19
    in American life, 91–93
    bots/popularity/fake news on, 99–103
    impact of, 103–4
    and Mitt Romney, 2
    political use of, 38, 38*t*
    president use of, 97–99
    revolution of, in Egypt, 21–22
    and roll call ideal points, 95*f*
    and tweeting to voters, 93–96
    use of, 30*t*, 34–36, 35*f*, 130*n*1
    viral on, 20–21

usapending.gov, 14
"User Guide and Codebook" (ANES), 56

Verba, Sidney, 19
verified accounts, on Twitter, 99–100
veterans, 128*n*18
viral, going, 2–3, 105
Voice and Equality (Verba, Schlozman,
    and Brady), 19
voters
    decision-making by, 57, 78
    turnout of, 68*f*
    tweeting directly to, 93–96, 96*f*
Vox, 101

Washington Post, 14, 64–65, 73
Watts, Clint, 101
Weiner, Anthony, 14
Wilmore, Larry, 58
Wireless Internet, 31
Wood, T. J., xvii–xviii
Word Press, 30*t*
Wray, Christopher, 97
Wray, Michael, 66

Yale University, 114
YouTube, 73–89
    about, 73–75, 129*n*3
    Clinton vs. Trump speeches on,
        86–87
    discussion bubbles on, 85–86
    and incivility/perception, 76–79
    and Mitt Romney, 1–2
    political deliberation on, 75–76
    and pussygate, 14–15
    real communication on, 87–89
    study of comments of, 79–85